LOSS OF BEING

To Rick
Best Wishes
Don N'Y
Feb 19, 2006

LOSS OF BEING

✦

Overcoming Despair in Modern Life

Don C. Nix J.D., Ph.D.

iUniverse, Inc.
New York Lincoln Shanghai

LOSS OF BEING
Overcoming Despair in Modern Life

iUniverse books may be ordered through booksellers or by contacting:

iUniverse
2021 Pine Lake Road, Suite 100
Lincoln, NE 68512
www.iuniverse.com
1-800-Authors (1-800-288-4677)

ISBN-13: 978-0-595-38003-9 (pbk)
ISBN-13: 978-0-595-82374-1 (ebk)
ISBN-10: 0-595-38003-4 (pbk)
ISBN-10: 0-595-82374-2 (ebk)

Printed in the United States of America

This book is dedicated to my two teachers, Hamid Ali (A.H. Almaas) and Faisel Muqaddam. With great gratitude for their care and attention, and for having had them both in my life.

Don C. Nix
Sonoma, California
November, 2005

Contents

Introduction

This book chronicles my encounter, in a time of spiritual crisis, with two teachers, Hamid Ali, (a.k.a. A.H. Almaas), and Faisel Muqaddam. They entered my life at a time when I needed help desperately. I was caught in a spiral of pain that I did not understand. I did not know what to do or where to turn. In the midst of my crisis, I stumbled into their work, seemingly by coincidence. I felt that they took my hand and led me, step by step, back to my depths and back to health.

I had been absorbed for decades in my progress in the world. I was accustomed to moving through life rapidly, and orbiting around issues of personal success and failure. I had given my spiritual life no attention whatsoever. Over time, I had lost touch with my depths and with Being itself. I realize, in retrospect, that this brought on my crisis.

When I look out into American society today, I see people moving so fast that they cannot think straight, let alone touch depth in life. Despair and emptiness appear to be universal. Popular culture is nihilistic, cynical and destructive. Our young people are lost in a miasma of confusion. Nothing clean and pure and beautiful is offered to them. I believe that there are millions of people in the society going down the same path that I trod, running fast but desolate in their need for meaning.

I put this book out into the society in the hope that the information will reach a few people who need it now as desperately as I once did. I hope to light a fire in such people, and give them the means to begin healing their consciousness. Our society is suffering from a great hole in consciousness where majestic, living Being should be. The result is despair, meaninglessness, emptiness, and alienation. Both as individuals and as a society, we need healing. Perhaps a ripple effect can be achieved, an "Each One Reach One" effect. Perhaps healing is contagious. Perhaps we can change the consciousness of the planet, beginning with ourselves. It's worth a try.

1

Descent into Darkness

In mid-1985, the bottom fell out of my stomach. This was the only way I could describe to myself what happened to me. Overnight, I fell from an ordered, pleasant life into a pit of despair. I was left achingly empty, confronting an empty Cosmos, and in extremis. It felt simply like the bottom had fallen out of my stomach.

We were living in Alexandria, Virginia. My wife and I were painting and selling paintings, as we had for the past fifteen years. We were not ascending to the high realms of the art world, but we were making a good middle-class living, and doing every day exactly what we wanted to do. And what we wanted to do was paint. Making art had become a pleasant, rather humdrum pattern, infinitely preferable as a life-style to practicing law and university teaching, both of which I had tried earlier. My development as an artist was predictable and unexciting but going well. There was always another rabbit to chase, another technique to master. Life seemed good and enjoyable. Things seemed normal.

Then, overnight, the bottom fell out. I was suddenly full of grief--simple, pure grief--and emptiness. I had not the slightest idea why I was feeling grief and emptiness. Nothing had happened on the surface of my life to cause this phenomenon. My life pattern was the same. I was the same person. My thoughts and attitudes were the same. Inexplicably, however, I was suddenly overwhelmed by a consuming sense of loss.

I began to go to the studio in the morning, sit in my chair in front of my painting all day, and alternately cry and sleep. I couldn't paint. I couldn't think straight. I was immobilized. I could only focus on a vast sense of loss. Grief welled out of my depths day after day. My wife thought I was having a nervous breakdown. I thought that perhaps she was right. I tried to get a grip. Nothing helped.

Then my situation took a dangerous, physical turn. I found myself in the hospital with a pulmonary embolism, a blood clot in my lung. The doctors were clearly concerned whether they could dissolve the clot without releasing it into my bloodstream where it could enter my heart. I realized that my life was on the line. With good medical care, the clot was eliminated, and I was out of the hospital in ten days. Six weeks later, however, I was back in the emergency room with a massive hemorrhage in my stomach. I lost most of the blood in my body, required transfusions, and again was on the cusp of life and death. I realized with a jolt that, in my depths, my organism was seriously considering dying. I was in bad trouble.

When I emerged from the hospital the second time, a friend from law school called to ask how I was. When I replied that I had never been worse, he said: "You'd better get yourself to Esalen. I just spent two wonderful weeks crying in the hot-tubs of Esalen, and it was fabulous! Perhaps you can find out there what's going on." A week later, we were on the airplane to California, headed to Esalen to see if we could find out what was wrong with me.

We stayed at Esalen for a year. After a month, we flew back to Virginia, sold our house, and moved to California permanently. Life at Esalen was full and endlessly fascinating. We sampled the smorgasbord of avant-garde ideas moving through the therapeutic community and, therefore, through Esalen—gestalt, psycho-synthesis, storytelling, maskmaking, Virginia Satir's sub-personalities work, Jungian imagery work and much more. We did the bodywork, massage, and movement disciplines from Tai Chi to free-form Ju-Ju dancing and drumming under the moon. However, through the entire year, I continued to feel empty and lost, rudderless and adrift. My life had lost its basic orientation. My state involved depression and I was dogged by continual exhaustion, so that getting out of bed in the morning was a major struggle. My experience continued to be loss, emptiness, and grief.

I decided that I was suffering from burnout. Burnout was the hot topic at the time. I went through the literature that detailed burnout as a psychological phenomenon, a physical phenomenon, a sociological phenomenon, or a phase in the male lifecycle. I learned that great numbers of American men hit a similar wall in mid-life. The pattern was widespread enough to have been documented. I had company.

The best book on the subject at that time was The Seasons of a Man's Life, by Daniel J. Levinson. In a major research effort that became the basis for Gail Sheehy's later best-selling Passages, Dr. Levinson documented a widespread phase of emotional disintegration that occurs in many men in their late forties or early fifties. It was during this same period, and as a direct result of Levinson's work, that the phrase "mid-life crisis" entered our language. I was 46. I was right on schedule.

The literature on burnout was comforting in one way. It demonstrated that I was not alone, that men from all walks of life were experiencing the same problems. However, diagnosis is not remedy. The literature contained not a hint of what to do about my condition. It suggested that I should just live through it. As an aside, the literature noted that many men die in this period, unable to unravel the puzzle that their life has become.

So, as we left Esalen for San Francisco at the end of the year, I felt that my problem was burnout, and that masculine burnout was somehow connected to the stresses of American culture. It seemed incontrovertible that it was being experienced by large numbers of American men, though many of them were hiding their experiences from family members, co-workers and friends. Burnout seemed to be the answer. It was only later, in retrospect, that I realized that burnout was a superficial and basically inaccurate answer. Burnout was a symptom of a deeper problem.

2

A Glimmer of Light

At this time, a friend at Esalen told me about a work-school in the Bay area where folks were engaged in deep, serious and sustained transformational work. We moved to San Francisco, joined the school, the Diamond Work of Hamid Ali, and began doing the work in a very serious way. Over the next ten years, it formed the centerpiece of our lives. It presented an alternative framework of reality, of which I felt initially skeptical. However, I tried to do the work faithfully. I had no better options.

At the time that we entered the school, there was no orientation or instruction for newcomers. We found ourselves sitting in lectures side-by-side with people who had been doing the work for fifteen or twenty years. No explanations or definitions were offered to bring us up to speed. We were left to grapple entirely on our own with the material in lectures that were dense and filled with unfamiliar terms and concepts. For some time, it was all a giant muddle.

I began to notice a lot of talk about essence, both in the lectures and among the older students. I determined to grasp this concept. Reading, listening carefully, and talking it over with my wife, I gradually understood that essence was central to the whole framework. Essence was some kind of living, intelligent field or substratum that was everywhere beneath the forms of the material world, including myself. Essence was in the space around me also. Essence evidently had recognizable qualities. With a little concentration and awareness, I was assured, I could detect its qualities as they flowed through me. These qualities included joy, compassion, strength, will, peace, power and clarity. Each had a characteristic color, and each carried a different sensation as it flowed through the body. At first, the experience of feeling essential sensations was beyond me. Gradually, I began to perceive something that was subtle but definitely there. With continued awareness practice, it became possible to experience essence clearly. Essence was described as part of the nature of Being, the ground of all life. Recognizing it and experiencing it in the body offered the possibility of contacting and directly experiencing Being itself. This was getting more interesting.

A second, related endeavor in the school reinforced these experiences. Awareness of the interior of the body was greatly encouraged and emphasized. We were told to sense our arms and legs, then add looking, then add listening. This practice was designed to wake one up and bring consciousness to full aliveness, full awareness of the body and full alertness in the present moment. This simple little exercise turned out to be quite powerful. With a little application, my body began to sensitize. I started to feel my interior experiences in a new and intense way. I began to experience subtleties of sensation that I had not experienced before. I started to feel my insides as warm, energetic, changeable, pleasurable and intensely alive. Things were going on down there that I had spent a lifetime overlooking. I realized that I had never before turned my awareness to the interior of my body. Now that I was doing so, there was quite a lot of intense experience there. It became easier with this new body sensitivity to experience the qualities of essence as they flowed through me. My skepticism waned. There were changes going on. There was definitely something to this work. I intensified my efforts to understand and grasp the nature of Being.

3

The Nature of Being

Being is a vast field of pure potentiality. It is the living, unmanifest substratum out of which everything arises. Every form in the world of appearances, and space itself, emerges out of Being. Being is the universal medium, eternal and unchanging, while the world of forms it produces is constantly changing. Being is the ground of existence. It is livingness, an ocean of livingness. It is a cosmic field of pure consciousness and pure awareness. It is pure intelligence, the principle of intelligence itself—discerning, knowing, and discriminating. It is the principle of truth. It is the principle of value. One metaphor for Being is gold, which can be fashioned into many forms—a ring, a bracelet, a necklace—but regardless of the form it takes, it retains its basic nature as gold. The ocean, forming itself constantly into individual but temporary waves, is another metaphor. Once you are aware of Being, perceiving it is similar to the experience of touching a tissue in your body. It is palpable and tangible. It has substantiality. It can be felt.

Being exists only in the present moment. It is living presence, unfolding itself as the world of forms from moment to moment. We usually think of ourselves in terms of linear time. Our identity depends on the past, our memories, and the self-images we hold in our mind. We think that what we are now comes from what we were yesterday. But yesterday is gone. It does not exist, so what exists now cannot come from it. The living moment that is now must come from something that exists and is generative in this moment. That something is Being, underlying and engaged in continually manifesting the world of forms that we see around us.

Being differentiates itself into separate, recognizable qualities called essential aspects. Each has a certain nature, a certain flavor and a certain experiential tone. Experiencing the aspects of essence (strength, will, joy, compassion, etc) is close to the experience of taste and touch, with inner rather than outer senses. When Being is experienced as essence, it suffuses the entire organism and becomes the very substance of who we are. It mingles with the cells and molecules, and perme-

8

ates the consciousness and body. An essential aspect is Being experienced in a particular way, with particular characteristics. Essential aspects flow through the body and nervous system constantly, but we overlook them because they are not included in the consensus framework of reality.

The aspects of Essence are universal. Everyone experiences them the same way. They are attractive to people, because they are attractive to the ego. When people learn about them, they want these qualities in their lives. Many people are less interested in pure Being, because turning toward it implies the eventual annihilation of the ego. This is repugnant to the ego. It is only very late in the process of transformation that the ego begins to long for its own cessation. Until that point, the ego resists essence and Being at every juncture.

4

Loss of Being

After a year and a half, I realized that I was no longer feeling grief and loss. My emotional life felt almost normal again. Some kind of healing was underway. I realized that I had not been suffering from burnout, or at least burnout was not the root cause. I had been suffering from **loss of Being**. I was suffering from loss of contact with the ground of life, leaving me trapped in alienated, barren isolation, cut off from the source of all meaning, depth and sacredness. I finally understood the genesis of my desolation and grief.

The West lost Being along the way. Over the past four hundred years, it put its faith in reason, and invested itself completely in the material world. Non-material levels and aspects of reality dropped away, and atrophied in Western consciousness. The West formed a consensus consciousness that leaves out the most crucial aspect of reality, Being.

Our cultural conditioning today conspires to keep us out of touch with this central core of reality—the reality that the Cosmos is one vast ocean of living, intelligent consciousness, within which humans, cultures, worlds and galaxies arise, live out their life-spans, and are re-absorbed. We are caught in a cultural downdraft that teaches our children, generation after generation, that we exist in a dead universe. As a result, we have lost our ground. We have become disconnected from the essential core of life. This connection with Being is, unfortunately for modern Western man, the source of all experiences of deep meaning, value and sacredness.

This hole in consciousness amounts to "**loss of Being**." Life without sacredness and meaning, life without awareness of being held by Being, is irredeemably trivial, fearful, unsupported, alienated, and empty. Modern Western consciousness perceives a universe that is material, dead and empty, made up of separate, unconnected parts, only a few of which are considered to be alive. The universe is perceived to exist only on the material level. It is viewed as without intelligence,

10

without awareness, and mindlessly unsupportive, if not implacably threatening, to human life. It is emptiness enshrined.

In a dead, empty Cosmos, we can only live lives that are fearful and void of meaning. In a context centered on human life as the highest reality, we are too small, too vulnerable and too threatened to live fully and deeply. Trapped in a destructive world-view and disconnected from the vast livingness all around us, the consciousness of modern Western man has become alienated, despairing, superficial, and sterile. We live now with unrelieved anxiety, a constant sense of dread and meaninglessness, and deep, unrealized longings for the living ground of Being.

There is no alternative to despair in a dead and empty Cosmos. The only question is how crippling the despair will be, and what measures will be taken to try to escape from it. Addictions of all kinds are the response in our society. Recovery of Being alone can rescue life from the joyless, fearful alienation that it has become, and restore the full range of the human experiences of joy, security, value, depth, and meaning. We must find a way to bring ourselves back into contact with the living reality of Being all around us.

5

Transformation and Hypnosis

Among the methods used in the school to change consciousness were stream of consciousness monologs, repeating questions, and visualizations. The monologs and repeating questions were typically done with other students in groups of two or three, and were used principally to bring awareness to the personal ego barriers obstructing the free flow of essence. I looked forward to the visualization exercises because, for me, they reached much deeper, and brought about much more change. Many times they produced inner experiences that I still remember twenty years later. With direct experience, they opened new spiritual possibilities, and allowed me to move deeper into my being in a non-threatening way.

From this good experience with visualization, I became interested in the possibilities of using hypnosis to facilitate transformation. When I began several years later to work with my own clients, I combined instruction on essence with the techniques of hypnosis. I was amazed at the results. Led forward by essential experiences in trance, clients traversed ground in six weeks or two months that had taken me four or five years.

Encountering new ideas is only the first step, and doesn't yet amount to, transformation. Only when the new framework is brought to life by personal experience does transformation occur. Actual experience validates or invalidates the framework.

Hypnosis is admirably suited to getting past the conditioned mind patterns of an old framework. Hypnosis stills the noise of the mind-stream, deepens and focuses consciousness, and, to a great extent, disengages the defense systems and deals directly with the deep mind. In trance, a person can be guided to specific essential experiences and have an initial experience that lays valuable groundwork. Once an essential experience has occurred in trance at the level of the deep mind, the habitual framework of reality becomes more amenable to change. Sensitivity to essential realities can be rapidly expanded. The deep mind, where the worldview is held, does not distinguish between experiences in the material world, which are, in any case, turned into images and thoughts, and imaginal experiences occurring in trance, wholly within the imagination. Both are ultimately mental. Both impact the inner experience of the organism, and both can be sources of transformative power. Over the past few years, I have been working with clients at the nexus of transformation and hypnosis. My experience has been that trance-work is an invaluable tool in opening perception of new realities that have Being at their core.

6

Sa'ada and Sha'qa

As I paid more attention to my consciousness, I noticed that I was in very different states from day to day, sometimes from minute to minute. One morning I would wake up feeling the presence of Being palpably in the space around me in the bedroom. The next morning I could not perceive it. Being was obviously not coming and going. My changing states of sensitivity made the difference. Then, I found a simple but satisfying description of my experiences—Sa'ada and Sha'qa.

Sa'ada is nearness to Being. Being is then accessible and available. It flows through the organism because of its proximity. As it flows, it emanates feelings and sensations inherent in its primordial nature—value, well-being, fullness, health, and joy. Everything appears to be in its right place and working optimally. The universe seems full and good, even intimate, a wonderful home for a human being. Depth, meaning and sacredness are accessible, easily present and flowing.

Sha'qa is distance from Being. Lack of proximity renders Being inaccessible. It cannot irrigate the organism with its gifts, the qualities of Being. Sha'qa is a state of contraction. Its effects are alienation, isolation, depression and emptiness. Sha'qa feels like the center has dropped out of life. Existence feels hollow and meaningless. Hopelessness emerges and reigns. Life feels like messy chaos, scarcely worth living.

We move back and forth along a continuum between Sa'ada and Sha'qa. We experience first one, then the other, in varying degrees. As our framework changes to make Being central in our experience, however, we have increasing experience of Sa'ada. Our station shifts toward a state of connection and contact with the universe, allowing us to enjoy its qualities. We become aware of its mystery and magnificence, and we experience its joy, depth, and beauty.

Sa'ada heals emotional wounds. As essence and awareness reach a wound, the associated trauma is transmuted into a simple memory of something that once occurred. The affect of the trauma evaporates. Sometimes this process is quite dramatic and life-changing, as it was for Joyce, a young woman I worked with a couple of years ago.

Joyce came to see me to deal with fear. Six years earlier, she had been brutally attacked, beaten and raped in a Northeastern city, by a stranger who was ultimately caught, convicted and sent to the penitentiary. Vivid images of the attack still surfaced in her mind at odd moments, and brought with it fear and strong body reactions. She wanted to change jobs and move to a nearby city, but fear made her reluctant to risk the move. We worked together for six months, using verbal instruction and trance-work to expand awareness of Being. During that time, we did not once deal directly with the attack. The emphasis was wholly on stimulating the perception of, sensitivity to, and experience of Being. Joyce was a good subject. Slowly and incrementally, her inner experience began to shift. The framework held in the deepest levels of her mind began to transform.

At the end of six months of sustained work, she felt strong, solid, and held by Being. Memories of the attack lost their affect. The fear and negative body responses associated with the trauma disappeared for good. The attack became a simple memory, something that once happened and could be recalled, but was unaccompanied by strong emotion. Sa'ada had pulled the fangs of the trauma. Healing had occurred. With fresh feelings of self-confidence, Joyce made the move into her new life several weeks later.

Most of us never endure a devastating experience such as Joyce's. Our traumas are generally more subdued. However, fear comes in many forms in all our lives, and can greatly compromise our life experience.

7

Ego

In the early phases of the work, there was a great deal of discussion about the nature of ego and its relationship to Being. I was familiar with the ideas of ego coming from Hinduism and Buddhism, which consider ego to be a problem, a false self that causes suffering. I was also familiar with the position of modern psychology, which considers a strong ego to be vital to mental health. On consideration, I realized that I had never clearly defined ego. I wondered if my ego and my personality were the same thing. I found that they were. Ego is basically patterned behavior that we mistake for the self. It is a set of mechanical, conditioned responses that we depend upon to get us through life.

Ego or personality is a useful, but limited, artificial construction, relying on strategies, behavioral devices and defense mechanisms to deal with the world. It is formed out of the earliest childhood memories, experiences, and object relations. Human developmental theory states that the ego is constructed after birth, built from the baby's experiences with its mother and others in the period between birth and four, the most crucial period of life. The ego attempts to use strategies adopted at three or four years of age in situations arising decades later. They rarely work well.

The ego masquerades as the captain of the ship, but is an imposter. Being steers the ship of life. The personality is only along for the ride. Ego is aware of its falseness and deficiency, but attempts to pose as Being. For every essential quality that is inherent in the field of Being, ego constructs a false counterpart. For example, where Being would generate essential compassion, ego, in trying to mimic compassion, succeeds only in generating sentimentality. The ego's substitute for essence is always a little off, and always feels somehow false.

Ego interferes with the flow of essence through the organism. It creates barriers from its various traumas, strategies and defenses. The barriers are by nature physical, emotional and mental contractions that prevent essence from flowing freely. Work must be done to make the barriers conscious and understand them, in order to free up the system so that essence can flow through and carry out its enlivening, life-ordering and life-maximizing functions.

Ego can be recognized by its mechanical and repetitive qualities. It has a knee-jerk response to situations. Based on memories and responses learned earlier, it is programmed and rigid. In similar situations, the ego will almost always respond in the same, inflexible way. Essence, on the other hand, is flexible and, in similar situations, may respond in completely different ways. This is because essence, generated out of the unity of Being, responds to the entire situation that is emerging at any given moment, including the needs, barriers, well-being and impacts on all persons involved. Essence always seeks the optimal.

The nature of the ego is that it creates two experiences: (1) the sense of separateness, or individuality, and (2) the sense of identity, the sense that you know who you are, the unique composite of characteristics that distinguishes you from everyone else. The developmental theorists, in tracking the development of the ego, have laid out for us the process of the formation of the false self, with its experiences of separateness and personal identity. All major spiritual disciplines say that the ego is a false self. We are struggling to see beyond it to our true nature and our true self, which is Being.

Without memory, there is no ego. The ego is based on a self-image held in the mind, a composite self-image that coalesces all the diverse self-images that come out of memories, mental pictures of the body, interactions and experiences at different moments in life. The ego is basically an illusion based on image and memory. The mind constantly reiterates and reinforces the false identity based on these images. In this image-based identity, characteristics are set. They remain consistent, all derived from memory. The problem arises in defining oneself as this limited ego structure. The spiritual problem is not that we have the wrong self-image. The problem is that our identity is based on empty images rather than something real, Being.

The goal of transformation is to loosen the tyranny of ego identity, and move beyond the experience of being a separate individual. This is completely incomprehensible to someone who has not done work in this area. It is not understood to be a possibility, or to make sense of any kind. Education must occur, and new ideas must be entertained. With growing awareness, it is possible to move beyond ego identity. The process usually unfolds slowly, over a considerable period of time. In a major crisis, however, such as a health emergency, it may happen rapidly. David's story, which unfolded in 2004, illustrates what can happen when transformation suddenly becomes crucial.

David received a diagnosis of metastasized prostate cancer a week before he attended one of my classes. He was an energetic, dynamic man in his late fifties, a lawyer who had started several successful businesses. At our first meeting, he was agitated and deeply troubled. He told me that he had spent his life whirling in the world, completely absorbed in his start-ups. He had never taken the time to turn toward his spiritual depths. We began consciousness work, using instruction, visualization, and trance.

It was evident immediately that he was desperate for a spiritual framework. He was parched and empty, threatened, fearful, isolated, and alone. He was a dry desert waiting for rain. I gave him an increasing number of trance sessions, instructional sessions, tapes and written materials, but he continued to ask for more. It seemed that he couldn't get the information fast enough.

As his condition deteriorated, he was in and out of the hospital and in bed at home. He used the opportunity to work almost full-time on developing his awareness of Being. Over a period of six months, he did the work of four or five years. He became able to perceive essential qualities in his body, and the presence of Being outside himself. With great courage and great awareness, he faced what was coming.

When he died, it was a peaceful death. He simply forgot to take the next breath. In our last times together, he said to me: "I'm getting it. I can feel Being inside myself and around me. Space is full of Presence. It's tangible and real. Why did I wait so long to begin working on my spiritual life? How could I have lived so long in that emptiness when this was available?" David died into fullness, a universe full of Being and Presence, a welcoming and holding universe, the antithesis of empty space.

David's story illustrates how powerful our absorption in ego can be. Unless we are somehow shaken into the realization that our time here is brief, we can go through decades or a lifetime without attending to our depths.

The ego is reactive, defensive and full of agitation. It is also stale. It brings memories of the past and superimposes them on the present moment. Based on images and the past, the ego has no ontological reality. Being, on the other hand, is alive in the present moment, generating life, and it can be experienced somatically.

The ego is not a bad thing. It is simply incomplete—an arrested development. We have uniqueness and individuality, but based in Being rather than in image. If transformational work is undertaken, and ego is allowed to continue its development, it will lead eventually to Being in individualized form, a real identity rather than a false one.

8

The Super-Ego

One of the most important parts of the work for me during the first couple of years was the work on defending against the super-ego. Until I did this segment of the work, I didn't realize how much I was continually devastating myself with this critical, internal voice. My personal history includes religious fundamentalism in my family. Fundamentalism is enforced primarily by shame. It is a ripe ground for the super-ego. My background left me with a particularly vicious super-ego. I had tried earlier to get a handle on it, but this was the first system that actually worked. When I saw that it worked, I got very excited. I spent a lot of time and effort vigorously defending myself against my super-ego. It paid off. Although I occasionally still have to defend, for the most part I have silenced my super-ego by using this method. It is a vast relief, and allows me to be more peaceful, more content, more self-compassionate, and more functional in the world. Life has more possibilities if you are not bombing yourself every minute.

The super-ego is the psychic structure that lays down standards for our behavior. It is formed during childhood through interaction with the parents. It could be described as an internalization of the parents, so that even if they are no longer present guiding and correcting behavior, they are still there as structures in the mind, doing the same job.

At base, the super-ego performs a healthy function. It socializes the individual and makes him fit to live in society, following the rules and living a life generally in harmony with the culture. The super-ego gives guidelines about right and wrong. It enforces ethical and moral behavior, generally by inflicting shame and guilt when the rules are transgressed or about to be transgressed.

The problem in adulthood is that the super-ego may get out of hand and become devastatingly hypercritical and shaming. It is common in our culture for the super-ego to sustain on-going criticism, constantly inflicting deficiency and shame. It can move to unceasing attack, destroying self-esteem, self-support, self-compassion and self-holding, leaving the individual dis-empowered, wounded and bleeding. Attacks of the super-ego are particularly devastating because the individual usually takes the attack message unquestioningly to be truth. The individual undergoing constant attack from the super-ego lives fearfully and essentially castrated. Attacks destroy will and capacity. Contentment, self-esteem, and any sense of well-being disappear. One of the most powerful examples I've seen of this was with a woman that I will call Denise.

Denise hated her body. She came to see me to work on problems of relationship. In her late thirties, she had had relationships in the past, but currently was without a partner, and wanted to find one.

In our first session, I determined that, before we took up other issues, she needed to work on the super-ego. She was being bloodied by her super-ego, which was telling her that she was fat and unattractive, that no-one could possibly be interested in her. Her mother had been harsh and judgmental about Denise's appearance, and it had left her with a particularly vicious super-ego. Every magazine that she picked up evoked self-hatred, as she compared her body to those of the models.

When I explained the possibility of defending against the attacks of the super-ego, she expressed hopelessness. She had been in pain since her early teens around her body image. But, she was willing to try.

It was hard work. The first stage was to train her to recognize the super-ego attack the moment it launched. In short order, she was able to do this. She became able to register the attack, and she could state exactly what was its message. The second stage was more difficult. It involved finding the energy to defend, or counter-attack, at the very moment when her energy was sapped by the attack. With work, she developed her own individual style of defending, a style that she was comfortable with and could repeat over and over.

In a few weeks, she reported that she was making progress. She was defending every time she perceived an attack, which was many times each day. The attacks began to come less frequently. When she saw that it was working, she re-doubled her efforts. The attacks continued to wane. After three months of effort, Denise said that the attacks were coming very infrequently. She also felt confident that, if one did come, she could stop it in its tracks. She discovered from her own experience that the super-ego can only inflict deficiency if it remains in the shadows, unseen, if its messages are accepted unquestioningly as truth. Two years later, Denise still has to defend occasionally, but body issues are no longer a major problem. It helps that she has found a successful relationship that continues to go well.

As Denise's experience shows, the super-ego is highly resourceful when it comes to finding subjects for attack. The subject matter may change from day to day, but the message of deficiency and inadequacy remains constant. The internal, critical voice may one day say: "You're unattractive. You're fat. You're getting old." Later it may say: "You're stupid. You're untalented. You can't do anything well." Another day it may whisper: "You're a failure. Nothing you attempt ever turns out well." There is never a lack of subject matter, because feelings of deficiency are generic to every ego. This generic deficiency provides wonderful opportunities for the super-ego to hang feelings of deficiency on one peg or another.

It is essential to build awareness of the super-ego's manner of attacking, so that the attack can be instantly recognized and defended against. Defending involves mobilizing the energy to turn toward the super-ego and fiercely resist the attack. "Get out of my head!" and "Get lost!" are possibilities for defensive statements. Using a little profanity will increase the energy thrown back at the super-ego. Defending promotes dis-identification with the super-ego. It objectifies it, so that when it swings into attack, it can be perceived and countered. It is necessary to get distance from this part of the psyche. It is hostile to our well-being, and attacks can seriously damage self-esteem. They can also destroy a sense of personal value. If work on defending against the super-ego is persistent and successful, attacks will diminish in frequency and intensity. It is sometimes possible, over time, to silence them completely.

9

The Point

Two years into the work, I was still coping with feelings of emptiness, both within and without. I heard from various quarters hushed conversations about "the Point." When I inquired about this, I was politely informed that it was very advanced and probably beyond me, since I was still a novice. Naturally, this increased my curiosity and my determination to find out more. After some nagging, I finally found someone willing to share the knowledge with me. It turned out to be vital to my healing. It provided the answer to the emptiness that had plagued my experience for three years. It was a crucial turning point for me. I have since come to believe that, rather than leaving the information on the Point until late in the teaching, it should be taught first. It is easily communicated, deceptively simple and profoundly transformational.

The Point is a living, eternal, indestructible point of light that resides within your heart, though it may move through the body. It is self-luminous, intelligent, and alive. It is an impersonal spark of the universe, a tiny, glowing bit of Being with all of the qualities of the Cosmos in it. The Point is an interface with Being. It connects the human to the universe, and makes available all the qualities of Being. It's a direct portal to the Absolute.

Another way of regarding the Point is as a tiny, living star, generating the light and life of pure Being. It is self-radiant. It glows by it's own livingness. It is Being in its purest, most concentrated form. A third definition of the Point is "the real self." This is the real self that consensus reality has forgotten. We are born in touch with it, but its existence is educated out of us. As we grow, our experiences and coalescing reality framework destroy access to it. The Point never goes away. We cannot be without it. We can and do, however, lose access to it. We become trapped in consensus mind. With no awareness of the Point, we define ourselves as material beings.

The Point can be seen in the mind's eye, glowing in the heart or elsewhere in the body, or sometimes even outside the body. Kinesthetic types who are less visual may experience it as a warm, intimate presence in the heart. Many people encounter it without knowing what it is. It can come in full waking, in dreams or in reverie. Sometimes the Point can be seen or felt in another person. With work, the Point can brought to awareness fully and permanently. The true self then becomes not the body, but the Point. The body is inhabited by the Point. Bodies come and go. The Point endures, and moves from body to body through many lifetimes.

Bodies are disposable. The circumstances of this lifetime are transient. What remains as the real self when the body drops away is the Point. It will move to a new body and continue its journey. The Point moves through the corridors of life, accumulating knowledge about the universe and the nature of reality. This is, in fact, the Absolute investigating the Absolute, to ascertain its own nature. We are participants in that vast inquiry.

This is a long process. The Point is in no hurry. It was never born. It will never die. It is eternal and indestructible. We spend our lives in search of it. The longing for it drives human behavior. That longing is transferred to material possessions, to relationships, to career, to ambitions, to hopes. Humans claw at the world trying to satisfy the longing, but none of the things that the material world offers will satisfy it.

Longing and feelings of incompleteness continue throughout life. The only thing that will assuage them is the assimilation of the Point. Once that is accomplished, the longings cease. Then it is possible to relax into life and just be along for the ride. It will be interesting, at that point, to see what's going to happen next. Death will cease to be fearsome. If identification is with the body as the true self, death of the body equals annihilation of the entire entity. If identification is not with the body but with the Point, death is just an event. The Point moves through it and proceeds with its journey.

When the recovery of the Point begins, there's a sense of coming home, a feeling that relaxation and peace are finally possible. The coming home is to Being and fullness, to reality, to the true self.

When the Point is recovered, it ends the waiting. There is a sense in life of eternally waiting—waiting for meaning, waiting for things to make sense, waiting for depth, waiting to become valuable. The waiting is actually waiting for contact with the Point. It is possible to spend a lifetime waiting, never knowing exactly what you are waiting for. Waiting is characterized by a sense that something is wrong, that a crucial shoe has not yet dropped. No alternative exists to waiting for meaning until the Point is recovered and reintegrated. Once this is accomplished, the uncomfortable sense of waiting vanishes.

With the Point intact, there is a feeling of security. The realization comes that nobody can harm you. At the deepest level, we are indestructible. The body can be harmed, but the real self, the Point, can never be. It's beyond harm. It was never born, it will never die, and it cannot be harmed. There is great solace in realizing this truth.

The experience of the Point is an experience of being a center of substantiality. There is finally somebody home. There is a core entity in the depths. The knowledge yields an experience of solidity. The statement is: "I exist. I am here. I am substantial. I'm to be reckoned with."

Having the Point also makes possible the experience of being a center of influence and power, being dynamic, making things happen. Lack of access to the Point, on the other hand, results in feelings of personal deficiency. Recovering the Point heals the experience of deficiency, as the following story of William illustrates.

William was the child of an abusive father. From early childhood, he had been physically mistreated and emotionally attacked. In his late twenties, he was fearful and lacked self-confidence. He had been a bartender for several years, but wanted to change careers and improve his prospects. He was full of feelings of personal deficiency, however, and felt reluctant to risk a change. We started instruction and trance-work on the Point and other issues.

William's feelings of inadequacy were deep, grounded in years of childhood experience. They did not yield easily. After several months, he began to talk occasionally about becoming a wedding and events videographer. He researched equipment and began to put together funds. At a deep internal level, there was a growing experience of solidity and substantiality coalescing around the Point. Though almost invisible on the surface, a shift was taking place from disabling inadequacy to self-confidence. Several months later, he put an ad in the newspaper and launched his new business. At last report, the business was going well, and William was fully occupied with his new endeavor.

Having access to the Point results in realizing that each of us is a center of thought and consciousness. Creative images and structures appear in the mind. They may be entirely unique, never having appeared to anyone else who ever lived. The Point is the genesis of this dynamic, creative consciousness.

Having the Point produces a sense of being here as an eternal entity, embedded in form, immortal and invincible. Suddenly, the lens shifts. Identification with the vulnerable body is a delusion that takes the part to be the whole. Recovering the Point is actually becoming whole. The picture completes itself. Identity with the Point at the center becomes a truthful portrait of a human being.

What are the experiences of not having the Point? We might call this projecting the Point. It involves looking for it in the outer world. In this society, we overlook the Point. Our children are not instructed in its existence, or how to make contact with it. So, we overlook it. It's missing in the reality framework. Every influence in the culture leads us to identify instead with the body.

Without awareness of the Point, we lose our real selves. Where a solid experience of selfhood should be, there is nothing. We are empty. We try to fill the emptiness from outside ourselves. We try to find the qualities of the Point in the world around us. We assume that it is possible to find something out in the world to hang onto, something that will give purchase. This does not work. The dynamism, depth, power and solidity of the Point cannot be obtained from the world or from other people.

One possibility is to seek the Point in relationship, trying to fill the emptiness with a spouse or a friend or a lover. It is possible to seek in others the qualities that we feel we lack ourselves. Projecting qualities of the Point onto the other person, we may feel that our life, survival, happiness and existence depend on them. We unconsciously feel that when they are with us, the qualities of the Point are present. When they are not, the qualities are absent. This is delusory. Our Point is never in another person. Its dynamism and living power are always inside of us. Witness the following example of Diane, who recovered her Point and its core solidity in very trying circumstances.

Diane's husband was dying of lung cancer. He was an instrumental man, used to making things happen and getting results. He approached his illness in the same way as he approached his business decisions. He threw all his resources at the problem. In the case of his illness, this meant obtaining the latest avant-garde, very expensive treatments. He made plans to spend large sums of money on his illness, sums that not only would wipe out their savings, but also put them deeply into debt. Diane needed to have her interests considered. If he spent their life savings in this way and then died, she would be left not only alone but destitute.

In their relationship of ten years, she had projected will and dynamism onto him, and he had projected compassion and nurturing onto her. Not only the unspoken contract of the relationship, but also the possibility of being seen as self-interested and unsupportive in his crisis, made it almost impossible for Diane to speak up, to get her interests considered in the crucial decisions that were being made.

In a series of conversations, however, she found the inner strength to ask that, in making the decisions, they take into account the possibility that he might not survive. If that turned out to be the outcome, she needed to be left in a position that she could survive without economic devastation. She found the Point in herself, and it contained the solidity and strength that she needed, that she had formerly projected onto him.

Her husband was, at first, shocked. Then he accepted it. He saw that her concerns were legitimate, and that, although he was certain in his own mind that the treatments would succeed and he could re-coup the money spent, there was a possibility that they would not. He eventually succumbed to the illness. Because Diane had put her own interests on the table, however, she was left in an economic condition that allowed her to continue her life. Her strength prevented her devastation.

It takes great fortitude to do what Diane did. Not everyone can find such strength when faced with the kind of dramatic life situation that she faced. Perhaps that is one of the reasons some people turn to groups or institutions to support them in difficult times. It is common to project the Point onto groups or institutions. Churches are prime examples. One may assume that wisdom and answers reside in the church. However, projecting the Point onto a church only results in its loss. The answers are never in institutions. When the Point is projected, in all cases it is lost. An empty void then exists in the individual where the Point should be. A crucial sense of self as a powerful entity, filled with Being, essence, strength and core livingness, is lost.

Psychology talks about this area as self-referral and object referral. If the Point has been projected and lost, object referral occurs. Cues are taken from the outside. Loss of the Point leaves the personal agenda inaccessible. Likes and dislikes become hazy and obscure. Loss of the Point can even leave a person out of touch with the needs of the biological organism. A person with no self-compassion, who works until they drop in exhaustion, has projected the Point. If the Point is intact, they will refer to their own organism to see whether they need rest. This is self-compassion in the form of self-knowledge. If the Point is intact, something will ask: "What's the situation? What is my condition?" When biological limits are exceeded without realizing it, it is due to lack of contact with the Point. Nothing intervenes to say: "You're tired, stop, sleep, rest." So, limits are exceeded to the point of exhaustion. That type of exhaustion is always a result of projecting the Point. The Point has wisdom and will take care of the organism. Without access to the Point, that wisdom is not available. It is possible, even likely, to lose one's bearings and get caught up in the whirl of life, as Peter, in the example below, did.

Peter was a refugee from Silicon Valley. He had spent several years of sixteen-hour days, seven days a week, trying to launch a technology business with partners. His work habits cost him his marriage, and were affecting his health. When the dot.com industry collapsed, his business bankrupted and he came to Northern California to try to start over.

When we began to work together, Peter was in a state of desolation and emptiness. He felt that he was a failure, that his life was meaningless, and that he had no future. We started to work in trance with the Point and with Being. Peter essentially had no spiritual history. His mind had never gone in that direction. He was, however, desperate to get relief from his desolation, and he was open to all possibilities. He was introduced to the Point and Being with instruction and visualizations. For some weeks, there appeared to be no change in him.

Then, over a period of time, he reported a series of dreams, in which he was driving a huge ocean liner and attempting to change its course. He struggled mightily with the steering wheel, which completely resisted him, until at last the ship began to change direction ever so slightly. In the dream, he felt elated and powerful at his success in influencing, even a little, the course of the liner. In successive dreams, he was able to change the ship's course even more. In still later dreams, he could steer the ship at will.

Emotionally, Peter's experience began to change. Inner emptiness and desolation slowly gave way to fullness. He became able to experience the inside of his body. The Point appeared in his mind's eye at odd moments. When he looked at nature, he could sense the presence of Being.

Some months later, Peter announced that he was leaving to launch a new business. He felt strong and competent again, and eagerly looked forward to the challenge. He appeared grounded, in touch with his Point and with his core. In taking his leave, he assured me that, in the future, he intended to put as first priority the needs of his organism.

Projecting the Point leaves us bereft of guidance. There is guidance available in the human organism, but only if the Point is intact. It alone is the source of objectivity and wisdom. It is the entity that tells us what the situation is and what needs to be done. If the Point has been projected, we are left with no internal system of guidance. Something must be there to guide, and that something is the Point.• A person will often seek guidance by turning to consensus reality images. These images carry information about how we should act and what we should be in the opinion of the society. The trouble is that today many of society's consensus images are full of sickness. Media images are often aimed primarily at stimulating consumerism. We have to be skeptical of consensus reality images. In this time period, they are not friends. They will lead us astray.

The Point is important in feeling personal value. We all long to feel valuable. If the Point is intact, value is naturally conferred. Being is the source of value. With no access to the Point, value will be sought in accumulating material possessions or achievement or notoriety. External sources of value, in the last analysis, never work for long. They may temporarily lift the spirits, but the feeling of value that they generate is fleeting.

If we don't go to images for guidance, we may go to rules. Religion used to serve this purpose. This is mostly defunct today, but religion used to provide rigid rules about how we must live our lives. The trouble with rules is that they are dead knowledge. Essence, Being, and livingness are right in the present moment. Trying to live according to rules requires mechanically sorting through them to determine which ones apply to the situation at hand. We never know if we have got it right.

Having a system of rules is an inadequate way of getting guidance. At best, it's dead knowledge that may not apply to the situation at hand. It looks in the wrong place to find an answer. Contact with the Point automatically supplies knowledge about what to do. It comes by way of intuition and flashes of insight.

Loss of the Point also keeps us from being real. Being real means being who we really are, even if people don't like it much. Large amounts of energy are tied up in repressing parts of oneself that would not be approved. There is great satisfaction in standing in the world as who one actually is. "Like it or lump it, here I am!" That's part of coming home. It requires a considerable amount of courage.

If the Point is not available, it is not possible to contact the real part of yourself, because there is no way to discern the real part. As a result, life is lived according to images of how one would like to appear to others. And, the shell is constructed. The shell is the dense, hard, exterior surface that we present to the world. It is essentially false and full of mechanical responses. It is the ego's version of the self, based on contraction, manipulation and effort. The loss of the Point keeps one from being real, and there is a resort to the shell as a substitute.

Without the Point, we have inadequate access to true will and true strength. The part is missing that would consolidate or coalesce to generate will and strength and yield confidence to act in the world. There's nothing to create a solid core, so the tendency is to reach outside for solidity. This produces shaky feelings about real capabilities. Beneath the shell always lie feelings of deficiency and fear.

Finally, we cannot truly experience transformation unless the Point is in place. Including the Point is necessary to a realistic definition of self. It's a fundamental component of transforming consciousness. Until the Point is recovered, we cannot get beyond the life of the ego. The Point gives us a place to stand in order to observe the ego. Absent the Point, ego is the only game in town. Once the Point is recovered, we can move beyond ego and see it as a necessary, useful thing to have, but not our true self. The ego has capacities to deal in the world, but it's only a tiny part of us. It is not the true self.

The goal is to move to identification with the Point. This is a requisite of transformation. The idea of deficiency is conjured by the ego. The ego knows that it is a false self, and feels its deficient falseness. If the Point is in place, we will not be conflicted about deficiency or value. Those questions will not arise. The Point will provide the answers. We are more than valuable. We are value itself. We are the latest product of 4 billion years of evolution. The Absolute has been working 4 billion years, evolving from single-cell organisms to multi-cell organisms with organs to development of species, to produce us. Here we sit as the latest model. We have no idea what's going to come next. We're along for the ride, and a magnificent ride it is.

10

The Point and Identity

Identity is the answer to the question: "Who am I?" or "What am I?" It is the basic way we describe ourselves, not only to other people but also to ourselves. It's a subject that is usually below the threshold of consciousness. We are born into a social context and the society instructs us how to identify ourselves. We do it automatically. We never turn and examine the question of how we know who we are. It is unquestioned. The truth is, however, that our understanding of identity may shift over time. The way that we identify ourselves, what we take ourselves to be, may change. The answer that we give to the question "Who am I?" depends on our level of understanding and transformation.

Identity unfolds in four stages. We start with the identity that we receive from the culture. This is the body, the personal history, and the personality, or ego. The material self is given great prominence in this society. The personality is taken to be the real self. If we live with this unquestioned assumption, the answer to the question "Who am I?" is: "I'm my body, my personality, and my personal history. What else would I be?"

The second level of identity is postulated by psychology. It says that we identify ourselves with mental images that we hold of ourselves. We are concepts and images in our own minds. We turn toward these images to remind us who we are many times each day. Those rare moments when our minds are not occupied with such images are called "simple awareness." The tapes in our mind turn off and we are just present and aware, with no mind-stream. We are temporarily not reminding ourselves of our personal histories, the kind of persons we are, how we got this way, or our names or faces or bodies. We are simply awake and fully aware, with an empty mind.

The third stage of identity is the Point. When we move past images and see that they are just images and not substantial, we may also see that images are dynamic. They cause behavior and suffering, but they are not real in the sense that Being is real. Image has nothing real beneath it. It is empty. With identity derived from image, we know ourselves as a constellation of insubstantial images. When we move to the Point, we move past images to true identity. The Point is eternal. It is always there, shining. The Point temporarily inhabits a body, but that body is not the identity. The Point has capacities to deal in the world, but these are not its identity, just a set of capacities. It journeys through time and space, but the journey is not its identity either. We are born to a particular set of parents, but they are not the identity. We have an unique and individual ego, but that is not the identity. These are all details of the Point's journey through time and space, not the identity. The identities that we take ourselves to be in the earlier stages drop away as we identify with the Point. Our entire perspective on the process of living changes as a result.

The fourth stage of identity is the Absolute. Separateness vanishes. It generally takes a long time to reach this stage. Consciousness has to be worked on for a long time to erase the barriers in the psyche that hold identity in the old, familiar ego place. When asking: "Who am I?" it is eventually possible to answer: "the Cosmos". This answer is not the result of mental gyrations. It wells out of the deepest being. It comes from assimilation of the truth that there is only one unified field here, one Being manifesting and dissolving, metamorphosing continually and eternally.

The assimilation of this truth produces Sa'ada, merger with the Cosmos. It is not reached only with the mind. The body, the heart, and the entire organism are also involved. The question of identity becomes a response of the total organism: "I am the Absolute."

The identity that the culture provides—the body, the personal history and the ego—holds us inside the consensus framework. Inside that framework, it is not possible to have a deep experience of soul. Experiences of essence may appear, but they will be outside the consensus framework, and will likely be overlooked.

Transformation is initiated by the opening of consciousness to a new identity. That opening is toward more complex, alternate realities. The consensus mind has no alternate realities. It's a single consensus reality. People in the culture agree with great certainty that what we see is all there is. The trouble is that most of reality is shrouded and hidden, and remains an unfathomable mystery.

Identity as images in the mind is also a limited and superficial answer, still firmly within the framework of consensus reality. It includes archetypes, unconscious material and symbolic constellations, all of which constitute a collection of images by which you know yourself. Altogether, the collection forms an amalgam that is the self-concept. The self-concept is constantly brought to mind and acted upon. We act according to it, and it impacts our life.

Moving past images, it is possible to see that mental constructs have been taken for identity. If the Point becomes identity, the realization becomes available that we are simultaneously beings of two worlds—both a celestial spark of the living cosmos and a material animal with aggression, ego, and an animal soul. Moving to identity as the Point opens the perception that we are each a fragment of the Divine. We are Being surrounded by Being. There is nothing here but Being.

The recovery of the Point proceeds in three stages. The first stage is contact. Attention must be directed to the Point. A place must be made for it, perhaps provisionally, in the framework of reality. Possibilities then open up to have experiences of it. This leads to awareness as the second stage. After personal experience of the Point, the reality of it may be accepted from your own experience. The final stage involves unreservedly merging with the Point and realizing it as the true self.

Identifying with the Absolute integrates the understanding that there is a single field of Being beneath myriad forms. The cosmos is intelligent, alive, loving, compassionate, and conscious. It is the source of the essential qualities that we can experience. There are no parts. There is simply Being.

What we call change is the metamorphosing of the cosmos. Standing in the Point, it is possible to watch the entire universe, including your own body, ceaselessly changing, metamorphosing moment by moment. Being, like a strobe-light, creates an entirely new cosmic reality each billionth of a nano-second. Each time it flashes out in creation, the template of manifestation changes and reality alters ever so slightly. Over time, humans come and go, continents come and go, worlds and galaxies come and go.

There is no possibility of being disconnected from Being. It is possible to be unaware of it, which causes suffering, but there is no place that is disconnected. Being is immanent everywhere. Appearances of separateness in form are delusion. The world as multiplicity is delusion. At a deeper level, multiplicity vanishes into one field of Being, metamorphosing eternally and taking form as the world of manifestation.

11

The Point and Idealization

Idealization of others is one way to project the Point. This is familiar territory. We all know this experience. It's a significant component of falling in love. It also occurs with others—parents, children, bosses, friends, public figures. The process of idealization is ceaseless. It seems to be an integral part of the human experience. It is, however, a mode of projecting and losing the Point.

Idealization is a kind of deification. The other person is considered as a little more than human, pushed into the idealized realm. In a sense, idealization is reaching for divinity. The result is to make the other person quasi-divine.

In the process, there is separation from reality. The other person is perceived as having qualities of the Point that are actually internal. The qualities are inaccessible because the Point in not available, so we try to get them from the outside. We see qualities of our own Point as the ideal qualities of the other person.

One definition of idealization is "forming an image of another person, not as they actually are but as we need them to be." Every person is a mixed bag. Idealization overlooks this truth, in an attempt to full a hole in oneself by importing qualities from another person.

The subject of projecting the Point is especially pertinent for women. In this culture, women have in the past been trained to relinquish the Point. This produces an intense longing, a reaching outward for value and power. Men also commonly project the Point. Their situation is not quite so acute, however, because different archetypes come into play in their upbringing. The training given to young women encourages them to look outside of themselves for power and dynamism. It's a primary way that women have been lumbered by the cultural givens.

Idealization of another person rests on need for a missing quality of the Point. It arises from attempts to overcome feelings of deficiency and lack of value. Only the Point can fill those holes. If the Point is not accessible, a reaching outward to fill them will not be successful. The projection of the Point is, therefore, a reaching for wholeness, a reaching for health. The self is seeking wholeness by idealizing the other person. It is trying to complete itself out in the world. That never happens. Wholeness lies only in contacting your own Point and having all of yourself.

There are two types of idealization. The first magnifies certain traits that are needed, for example, power. A person who feels personally lacking in power may be drawn to someone who appears to exercise dynamic will in the world, who possesses an ability to make things happen. Idealization is an impulse to co-opt that quality, to share vicariously in the power. We use each other in many different ways: to get narcissistic supplies, to fill holes in ourselves, to attempt to make ourselves more complete. Sharing qualities is illusory, however. The other person's power and capability never become yours.

Another type of idealization omits traits that are unattractive, that don't fit with the idealized image. Traits become invisible in this way. If later they appear, it may be astounding that they were not noticed earlier. This is also a form of delusion. What is actually there and quite apparent is not perceived. One of the most common places that this occurs is in relationships, as in the case of Leslie, below.

Leslie did not do well with relationships. She had been married four times, and her current marriage was foundering. She was desperate to find out what was wrong. As she went though her personal history, a pattern emerged. With each marriage, a negative trait had emerged in the other person after marriage. Each time, it was a trait that she felt she could not live with. In one case, it was uncontrollable anger. In another case, it was an erratic, unstable emotional make-up. Another husband was so narcissistic that other people were only two-dimensional props, a stage-set, to his center-stage performance.

With each relationship, Leslie was surprised by the emergence of the flaw. "Why didn't I see that?" she asked repeatedly. Her friends had perceived it, and sometimes had shared their perceptions with her. As we worked with the Point, she gradually realized that she had little contact with reality around relationship matters. She was lost in idealization. She idealized each partner, in the initial phases of relationship, to the extent that she was unable to perceive them as they actually were. Instead, she perceived what she needed and wanted them to be. Inevitably, as reality asserted itself, she found herself in an unsustainable situation.

The healing for Leslie was awareness. Once she saw clearly the process of idealization and its results, she could act in a different way. She had to see her idealization at its inception to avoid being overwhelmed by it.

A person may be more than the image that is perceived of them, more expansive or more whole than the idealized image. In the distortion of the idealization, certain traits may be magnified and others omitted. Real parts of them may become temporarily invisible, and qualities that are not there may be fabricated.

Idealization rests on an ego experience of deficiency. It comes from childhood experience with the parents. It is a normal and necessary phase in child development. At an early stage, the parents are magical creatures to the child. The diaper is wet and it magically gets changed. Hunger occurs and food magically appears. The child needs to see the mother as magical because it is vulnerable and dependent on the mother for survival. The idealization of mother is necessary for this vulnerable little being. It doesn't have the mental structures to deal with reality itself. To survive, it needs an ideal, protected world for a certain period of time.

Later, painful experiences build up. Idealizations begin to crack. Eventually, the child splits the mother into the terrible mother and the good mother. The split is necessary to retain the good mother part of the idealization. The terrible mother is split off, leaving the good mother intact and perfect. A bit later, it is not possible to maintain this idealization and it also breaks down. The mother is then seen as less than ideal. She is perceived to be, like other human beings, full of holes, flaws and her own set of problems.

At that point, the idealization may switch to the father and start the whole process over. Later on, that idealization will also break down. As the idealizations of the parents erode, the qualities that were formerly projected onto them are internalized. This is part of the process of becoming an autonomous, adult human being.

In a normal psyche, the breakdown of idealizations happens slowly. Over a period of years, it is slowly realized that these people are not ideal. Indeed, in some places they're seen to be defective. When the breakdown takes place slowly, there is time to integrate into oneself the qualities formerly projected onto them.

The process is disrupted in some people. If the breakdown of idealization is too sudden or disturbed, it can result in problems. If a psyche has been constructed around an idealization that breaks, the sense of loss can be devastating. The breakdown of idealization can feel like a major cracking of the universe. Since the breakdown frustrates personal needs, feelings may range from mild disappointment to rage and betrayal. Health lies in eventually allowing the other person to be an ordinary human being, with ordinary human flaws.

When idealization breaks down, the tendency is swing to devaluation. Traits are devalued in the movement from idealization to devaluation. It may be carried to an extreme, where nothing good can be seen in the person. Over-reaction is common. It is the result of substantial disappointment that arises when the idealization cracks.

A healthy person, having gone from idealization to devaluation, will eventually see that this is also not accurate. The other person may not be the best of humans, but they are not the worst either. The healthy person moves to center and concludes that they are, like all others, flawed human beings. They are neither the idealization nor the antithesis of the idealization. They possess both good and bad qualities. They drive you crazy and make you joyful. At moments you love them, and at moments you hate them. The healthy person will wind up in the middle, finished with polarity tennis.

One definition of maturity is to adjust to these disappointments. When idealizations break down, it may be an opportunity to see the person, for the first time, in all of their humanity, reality and complexity. With idealization in place, it is not possible to be in touch with a complete person, but only with a part of the person, a distortion. A major goal of transformation is to perceive reality as it actually is, without distortion.

One component of the self-concept is the idealized self-image, an image of oneself as one would like to be. At moments, it may be assumed that the idealized self-image is actually who one is. It has been earlier selected, refined, and referenced as the source of worth and value. It is composed of images, archetypes, and personal qualities found attractive and selected when young.

The attributes may have been consciously chosen. The idealized self-image is an archetype chosen as a goal to grow into. Energy and effort may have been put into developing its qualities. They may now be a source of pride. They may be considered now to be the best part of the self.

The idealized self-image is often generated by the opinions and messages of the parents. Early on, the parents send the child messages that they approve of certain qualities. They encourage the qualities whenever they appear in the child. The child begins to mold itself around the images and archetypes that contain the qualities. Later, that child may spend its life trying to embody the idealized self-images. At the end of the day, however, these idealized self-images are insubstantial as identity, no matter how dearly they are held.

One function of the idealized self-image is that it counter-balances the attacks of the super-ego. When the super-ego attacks with its messages of deficiency, we may go to the idealized self-image to compensate. In this way, the idealized self-image may become a refuge from super-ego attack, Functioning like a thermostat, this process may be an attempt by the organism to maintain equilibrium, to avoid being swamped by super-ego attacks. Self-esteem can be supported and protected by the idealized image.

At some point in the process of transformation, it is important to face the fact that the idealized self-image, like other images, has no substantiality, no essential reality. Giving up the idealized self-image or having it cracked is usually very painful, particularly if it is cracked under attack. Family members are usually aware, at some level, of the content of the idealized self-image. They can often launch attacks with deadly accuracy at the idealized self-image. They know exactly where they can deliver the most pain.

There comes a point where the idealized self-image is no longer needed. Consciousness evolves to a point where the idealization is expendable. It is possible to grow past it and consciously bid it goodbye. This is a necessary part of transformation because, at bottom, the idealized self-image is false. Transformation involves growing toward true, essential reality. In any case, the deconstruction of the idealized self-image should be done slowly, carefully, and with great self-compassion, because every incremental loss of it is painful.

Joan, for example, in her sixties, was having trouble with one of her knees, and her energy level was low. Her good friend, Camille, asked Joan to co-lead a women's tour to China. Joan's way would be paid. The trip would cover several Chinese cities in a period of two weeks. Joan's first response was to take it on. She wanted to help her friend, she was intrigued by the thought of experiencing China, and it was free.

As she thought about it, however, Joan saw that she was acting on the basis of a self-idealization, an image of herself as totally competent, able to do anything, that belonged to an earlier stage of life. She saw that, in the grip of the idealization, the problems with her energy level and her knee vanished from the screen of her consciousness.

Once she saw the self-idealization, she was able to push through it to reality. She called Camille, explained her situation, and tactfully refused the offer. When Joan laid out her reasons, Camille took the refusal with good humor. Later, Joan said: "I felt that I reached the solid ground of reality. Although there were several reasons that I would like to have done it, I saw that, without the idealization, the reality was that I was not able. I saved myself a great deal of pain and anguish by seeing my reality clearly and refusing."

As Joan discovered, releasing self-idealizations is pre-requisite to contacting reality. There is resistance and fear around this process. Because idealizations and self-idealizations are structures in the ego, the ego may view this as dismantling one's life. There may be a feeling that the dismantling is too costly, that the idealization is too necessary. This is probably not true. Idealizations are generated by needs for essential qualities. The Point provides all of those qualities. It is not necessary to claw at the world or at other people to obtain them. They are available within. Being has every quality needed.

If the de-idealization process is handled slowly and with great awareness, it need not be disruptive. It's a matter of addressing it carefully, seeing how separated from reality it is, and moving toward reality a bit at a time.

Moving past idealization is groundwork for existing in the moment, for being real, and for seeing others as who they actually are. In touch with reality, it is possible to relate to others in a workable way. Idealizations often cause conflict. Relating to a person as an idealization, rather than as who they actually are, leaves part of them invisible. The invisible part may cause problems. Seeing a person as they actually are is pre-requisite to interacting with them realistically. Relationships are complicated, multi-dimensional, and difficult to keep on track. Trapped in idealization, one is vulnerable because out of touch with reality. If idealization can be moved past, it becomes possible to perceive a real person, struggling to survive, flourish, and find his or her way. We're all in the same boat. We're all incomplete, doing the best we can. Each of us is hampered by our shortcomings and by our delusions as we go along.

Breakdown of idealization creates an opening to reality and Being. The Point assists us in overcoming the ego's fear that it cannot tolerate the destruction of idealization. Without idealization, we can move closer to Being. The rewards of Being—joy, value, will, strength, compassion, power, and clarity—are the rewards of contacting reality just as it actually is.

12

The Point and Mirroring

Emptiness is the result of projecting the Point. The emptiness may take the form of being unsure about identity. If the Point is the true self and it is not available, how could the true identity be known? A crucial piece of ourselves is lost when we project the Point. At the extreme, this loss can produce the feeling that one does not exist. In a way, it has a grain of truth. The true self is not to be found in the framework within which life is being lived. In this case, it is necessary to look outside for confirmation of existence and value, for guidance, strength, will and solidity. It seems that emptiness could be filled with something out in the world, so we pursue the solution out there.

The Point is involved in mirroring. Mirroring is defined as being seen and appreciated for who we really are. It is being acknowledged and deeply understood. The individual psyche experiences a craving to be mirrored—to be seen, appreciated, and understood accurately.

This craving can be observed in young children. It is operative when they demand that their parents look at them, watch them perform, see what they can do. The need for mirroring attention goes on throughout life. We long for attention from our spouse, from our friends, from our boss, from almost everybody in our life. This craving for attention can be easily observed in oneself. We want to be seen and appreciated. In a group, we want to be noticed, seen and valued by the group. The longing is always present in human life.

When there are deficiencies in childhood mirroring, it is the cause of later suffering. Isolation and alienation can be produced by the impression that one is not seen, that no-one cares, no-one is paying attention. It can produce conflict in friendships and intimate relationships. The feeling of not being seen can produce emotions ranging from mild disappointment to rage. The truth is that we are rarely seen in the way that we want to be. In fact, we may wish not to be fully seen. However nice it is to have seen the pieces of yourself that are admirable, it might be uncomfortable and embarrassing to be seen warts and all.

In a marriage, both partners are usually so tied up in their own self-referencing that neither adequately mirrors the other. At the very moment that a partner complains: "You don't see me," that person is probably not seeing the other in all their complexity.

We spend a large portion of our energy searching for narcissistic supplies, among them mirroring. We try to manipulate situations so that people will pay attention to us and feed back positive impressions of us. This feels necessary, almost like food. When we do a good job, we long to have the results seen. We want someone to know about our efforts and our success.

It is a little shocking to become aware of this craving for mirroring. It is shocking to observe how much of our behavior is aimed at getting narcissistic supplies. The craving for applause and appreciation generates the urges to be famous and rich. The drive for status is, at bottom, a longing for mirroring and approval. Many people dedicate their lives to trying to satisfy the craving through career success, high performance, or fame. They never see the dynamic that runs their life. Beneath the sirens of the changing external goals is the impulse to be seen. It is assumed that achievement in the world will satisfy the craving. Ultimately, however, the craving cannot be satisfied from the outside. It may do so temporarily, but the craving is constantly re-born. It renews itself continually.

The origins of the craving for mirroring are in the early interactions with the parents. The child arrives in this realm fresh, unformed and new. The child does not yet know if it actually exists. It does not know whether it has value. It craves to be seen by the parents to confirm that it exists and has value. It wants its unfolding and growth to be witnessed by the parents to confirm that the unfolding is really happening, that the skills that it is putting together are truly being assembled. Once the parents see and confirm the achievements, the child can relax and get on to the next challenge.

In contrast to the child, the parents are large, solid, fully developed and fully in this realm of forms. The child perceives the parents to have the Point and its qualities. It is essential in raising a child to confirm for the child that it has its own Point, its own independent being. Sometimes the parents do this adequately, not because they know about the Point, but because they have an intuitive feeling that it is necessary and beneficial.

Other times, however, the parents are unconscious or narcissistic. They send the child the message that only they have the Point. The result is castration. This produces an adult who has been carefully trained out of possessing their own Point. They will live their life projecting the Point. Mental structures are created that deprive the adult of access to its own strength, will, initiative, intuition, personal guidance, all the emanations of the Point. The emanations of the Point flood through the organism only when the Point is intact. When there is no access to the Point, it is essential to recover it, so that emanations of the Point can flow. This can show up in many different ways. One of the most common is indecisiveness. I observed this pattern, and the transition out of it, in a woman named Rose who came to see me several years ago.

Rose was forty-three years old and full of uncertainty. She was unable to make decisions, even crucial decisions, about her life. She was unable to bring consideration of options to a close and take action. As a result, her life was in a shambles. Issues tended to pile up, one on top of the other, none of them resolved. If she had had a strong-willed husband, she might have used his will to get along in life, but she was on her own. She came to see me in agitation, and with considerable awareness of the source of her problems.

Rose was the daughter of loving but strong, domineering parents. As a child, she had been tightly controlled. All decisions were made for her. She was never allowed to experiment and fail, as failure at any task was anathema in the family. In addition, the parents held a strong, idealized image of who she should be, and who she was going to be in the future. Rose was expected and required to fit into the idealized image rather than investigate whom she might actually be.

She emerged into adulthood with a wounded will and diminished self-confidence. She was without the self-support to manage her life effectively. There was an empty hole in her structure where solid entity should reside. We began work on the Point.

Several weeks later, Rose reported a small lift in spirits. When I pressed her to describe it, it turned out to be not happiness, but a tiny, new feeling of instrumentality and capability. We continued to work.

Three months later, Rose arrived at our session in high spirits. She told me the following story: "I was sitting at my desk dreading to make a phone call about my house insurance. I did other things at my desk and put it off as long as I could. When I could no longer avoid it, I suddenly looked at my hand and said to it: 'Pick up the phone and make the damn phone call!' And, my hand did. When I put the phone down, I felt elated. I've felt elated ever since. I took dominion over my hand. If I can take dominion over my hand, I can take dominion over other things as well." She laughed. She was on her way.

Sometimes a shift in a seemingly small trait like indecisiveness can yield big rewards. Occasionally, it ushers in a way to live in a completely new and more satisfying manner.

The craving to be mirrored is at bottom a longing for the true self, the Point. After disconnection from the Point in childhood, the longing is transferred to other people and the outer world. In touch only with our false self, we want the image of that false self to be reflected back to us. So, we are mistaken on two counts. First, we long to see our true self. Other people are irrelevant if we are ourselves in contact with our true self. Second, the longing is to see the true self, not the false self.

Awareness of the Point ends this pattern. Contact with the true self is the final goal for which the craving is generated. Seeing the true self makes the longing disappear. The outside world is not needed to confirm that one exists, has value and is journeying through time and space. Inner experiences may be shared with someone else, but there is no grinding necessity to have them seen by another person.

The Point is your witness, and that is adequate. Your successes, trials and tribulations are witnessed by the Point. This is the true mirroring. The Point sees and appreciates your unfolding. It recognizes the hard-won qualities assembled through living and suffering. It notes progress. At this juncture, experience deepens, and the process of living takes on new dimensions of meaning. A more mysterious and more lovely universe opens up.

13

The Point and Orientation

The Point is the North Star of our life. In order to function as a human being, we must be oriented. It is necessary to know where we are, who we are and what surrounds us. Orientation is so fundamental to functionality that it is almost invisible. Autism results when children cannot properly orient themselves in time and space. If they cannot understand what is happening and how they are related to the shifting environment, they are non-functional. They cannot negotiate the world.

We carry orientation with us, not only about how to move in the world, but also about who we are and the system in which we are embedded. This is orientation at the most primordial level. It includes identity and constructs of reality. Orientation answers questions for us about what is real in the world.

The consensus mind in this culture is oriented to materialism and mechanism. Our culture says that the material world is what is real. If it exists in three dimensions and has form and materiality, then it is considered real. The second idea, mechanism, comes from Isaac Newton's time. It is basic to the old physics, now being replaced by the new knowledge and metaphors of quantum physics. The Newtonian view is of a physical world that is mechanical and works something like a clock. Material things collide with each other, and energy is transferred between them. Causation unfolds in the manner of billiard balls colliding. The human body is also viewed mechanistically. The heart is like a pump and the lungs are like bellows. The brain is similar to a gasoline engine, an electro-chemical machine that works by firing off tiny explosions. In every case, the metaphor invokes mechanism. The idea of mechanism captured the imagination of the Western world 400 years ago, and is now dying. It is no longer adequate as a framing concept.

We know from quantum physics that, at the level of particles, there is nothing here but flashes of light with information and energy in them. We see a solid, physical world because our sensory apparatus exists at this particular level. Looking down into the sub-atomic world with an electron microscope, nothing appears solid. It is space. The ratio of space to particle is about the same ratio as between the galaxies in outer space. It is true to say the world of forms is material, but it is equally true to say that it is immaterial. It depends on the vantage point. The culture's pre-occupation with material reality becomes more and more questionable.

The ego mind is absorbed in problem solving. Problem solving is a mental focus that derives from the survival instinct. It's powerful, useful, and necessary. We have ongoing problems to which we must attend. However, the list of problems to be solved keeps growing. If we solve one, another goes to the head of the list. The problem solving function can easily expand to fill all available consciousness. At three in the morning we may awake to worry about old age and death. If we don't worry about that, we may worry that the house needs to be cleaned tomorrow morning. The mind-stream brings one problem after another forward to grind on. This can proceed for a lifetime, unless we can find some way to alter the process.

The problem-solving process is powerful because survival fears fuel it. The process rests on a conviction of vulnerability. We feel that we must think hard about how to handle things to avoid being threatened. Survival may not actually be involved now, but the basic process, formed for survival purposes, continues to operate. If a present problem does not appear for consideration, then a future problem is selected. The future holds an infinite variety of possible problems to worry about. Thinking about the future, the contours of the problem can't be seen because they don't yet exist. For the same reason, nothing can presently be done about it. Future problems present needless sources of limitless suffering. The solution is to put awareness firmly in the present moment. Being exists in the present moment, at the moving point of the now. Being does not exist in the future or the past. Being moves from moment to moment unfolding itself. It doesn't plan. It just unfolds the next reality. It's difficult for the human mind to stay with it because it moves forward every instant into the next instant. The instant that we try to freeze reality in order to understand it, or to be more secure, we lag behind the moving point of the now.

The orientation to materialism and mechanism and the habitual colonization of consciousness by problem-solving occupies all our available consciousness. The process is agitated, full of anxiety and pressure. There is no peace. There is no mental space to experience essence and Being.

This process must be dealt with internally. We cannot stop it by dealing with the outer world. The process continues regardless of circumstances. Consciousness must be addressed in order to detach from anxiety and problem solving. Anxiety is paramount because materialism and mechanism are inadequate as an orientation upon which to construct our lives.

The orientation is false and non-supportive. With this orientation, we are cut off from Being. There is only one source of support available to us, and that is Being. The nature of Being is to generate life and support it. Feeling weak, threatened, fearful, vulnerable, overwhelmed, and unsupported in the world is the direct result of being cut off from Being. With Being held in the forefront of consciousness, support will emerge.

Orienting toward Being rather than material and mechanism makes the Point the central factor in our life. It brings life into line with basic reality. Material is the dying end of idea, the disappearing phase of Being. Things deteriorate in the material world. They go away, fall apart, erode and disappear. The material world is the final stage before disappearance into the non-manifest. The material realm is incomplete to serve as the center of our orientation.

We must construct an orientation that will allow us to be fully human, to completely fulfill our potential. We are designed for support by the universe. With Being as our North Star, with the Point in place, an alignment finally occurs where everything makes sense and feels right. The confusion and distortion that accompanies orientation to material and mechanism vanishes. The experience of emptiness is replaced by delicious fullness, both within and without.

With the Point at the center of orientation, there is a sense of belonging in this miraculous field of Being. We can objectively observe the working of ego from the perspective of the Point. Personal wounding and its results can be viewed in an objective and dispassionate way. Ego structure becomes transparent and understandable. Possibilities for transformation open up, and new options appear.

With the Point as orientation, there is a growing ability to distinguish between objective reality and delusion based on concepts and projections. A sense of awe and wonder appears. The orientation toward Being and the Point allow the universe to present itself in all its miraculous reality.

Orientation to the Point can be encouraged by constantly bringing the Point and Being to mind. This practice is called remembrance. Mental repetition builds new neural pathways. Remembrance will gradually change orientation from mechanism and materialism to Being. Being will become more central in consciousness. The adversary in this process is the ego. The ego is always agitated, always overwhelmed, always too busy to practice remembrance.

The ego will do everything it can to interrupt the process, because it is threatened by a reorientation to Being. It knows that, ultimately, it will be dethroned by the process. The resistance of the ego is a given, and it has many tools at its disposal. For instance, in this culture we are narcotized by busyness, and busyness favors reconstitution of the ego. Busyness is the primary way that people in our society go unconscious, and revert to habit and conditioned patterns. Clarity and will are constantly needed to battle the unconsciousness produced by busyness.

14

The Lataif

The Lataif, a gift of the Sufis, is a portal to Being. In the school, it was taught to beginners early because, with a little awareness and application, it is possible to begin experiencing it in the body. Lataif work involves learning to sense the aspects of essence as they flow from the field of the Cosmos through the body. Each aspect is a distinct quality of Being, has a particular color associated with it, and generates an identifiable somatic experience.

Once I grasped that we exist in a living field of Being, every cubit of which is conscious, intelligent, and possessed of qualities, I opened to the possibility of perceiving those qualities with my cells as they moved through my body. And, it began to happen for me. My experience moved from a mental framework to somatic, physical sensations. My body started to validate the concepts of the teaching. By this point in time, my native skepticism had waned. The work had already transformed my life experience. There was more to come.

The Lataif is similar in some ways to the chakra system of Hinduism. It posits a set of subtle organs in the body that act as interfaces between the individual and the Cosmos. Through the operation of these subtle organs, the qualities of living Being, the essential aspects of Being, flow through and become accessible to the human being.

The organs are five in number: Sirr, Akhfa, Qalb, Khafi, and Rouh. Each accesses a different unique, irreducible characteristic of Being. When activated, each center opens a particular state of consciousness. Each is located at a specific place in the body, and each is associated with its own characteristic color or photism. Altogether, the Lataif emerges to provide the qualities that we need to live our lives fully and well: strength, compassion, joy, power, clarity, and will.

In a healthy individual, the essential aspects flow through without hindrance, each arising as needed and departing to make way for the next. However, contractions may have been formed in the mind, body or emotional make-up, as a result of trauma, personal history, or life experiences. Having been hurt or wounded, the individual squeezes himself tightly in the contracted areas. Barriers are formed that prevent the free flow of essence through the system. Access to an essential aspect may be blocked or restricted, denying the organism the benefits of that aspect. The ego, ever active but with severe limitations, then formulates a distorted substitute to use in place of the missing essential aspect. The ego substitute is always a poor and ineffective imitation of the missing essential aspect. An example would be an individual who, lacking access to the essential aspect of strength, manifests anger instead.

The Lataif resides in a non-Western cosmology very different from the consensus framework in the West. The Cosmos is conceived as a field of living consciousness and intelligence rather than dead, empty space. It is regarded as an ocean of pure potentiality, with the material world emerging from the depths of that dynamic potentiality. The entire ocean of Being contains qualities or characteristics that are experienced as the aspects of essence. Since humans are inside the field of Being, its nature is our nature. Its qualities become our qualities as they flow through us from the field.

The Lataif offers direct access to Being. The availability of essential aspects depends on developing awareness, so that their passage through the body is perceived. It is not sufficient to entertain the aspects as a concept, or an interesting mental artifact. Nothing happens in this case. The aspects of essence must be integrated sufficiently to actually experience them in the body. New levels of awareness must be developed and sharpened. In our culture, we are trapped in the head. We do not expect to contact spirit with our body. It is necessary to entertain this possibility seriously enough to learn how to do it. It is as though the cells wake up. The nerve endings that are the inner sensing organs in the body wake up. They become able to perceive sensations arising in the interior of the body. With practice, the sensations differentiate themselves into the various Lataif aspects. Once this stage is reached, and the essential aspects are personally experienced coursing through the body, skepticism disappears. A panel of Nobel Prize-winning scientists could not convince one that it is just imagination. Knowledge becomes rooted in personal experience. This is the threshold of perceiving a new universe and a new experience of living.

The Lataif emerges from the substratum of unmanifest Being that underlies the material world. In an earlier stage of the world, all humans had access and awareness of this unseen layer of reality. Indigenous peoples had it, and in some cases still do. In the West, however, over time, our perceptions of this subtle and refined realm atrophied. We lost our sensitivity to Being, which exists beneath the material world, as the crucial core of reality. Having now become acculturated to the reductionist Western framework, Being is no longer available to us. There is a yawning empty hole where Being and essence should be in our awareness.

The Western framework does not associate emotional states with consciousness. The focus is rather on content of consciousness, the torrent of thoughts and images that make up the mind-stream. Consciousness is not conceived to have innate qualities—strong consciousness or compassionate consciousness or loving consciousness. Those qualities are assigned to the emotions, as the body's reactions to thoughts in the mind-stream. With Being put back in at the center of the framework, however, these emotional qualities become aspects of consciousness, aspects of Being, part of the ground of life. The aspects of essence are available to us, but only if we are willing to entertain reality outside the contemporary, shrunken Western framework. The possibilities of enrichment are there. By refining awareness, the essential aspects can be perceived as they flow through and enliven our life.

15

Red Essence

Lataif work begins with red essence, which is strength. The strength of red essence is needed to do the rest of the hard job of transformation. Transformation of consciousness involves nothing less than moving into a new framework of reality. This is not accomplished quickly or easily. When psychodynamic work is coupled with spiritual work, however, mountains can eventually be moved. Inevitably, the process throws up unconscious material that is unpleasant or scary. At these times, red essence provides the support to persevere and continue the effort. Red essence generates the primordial strength that we need, not only to transform our consciousness, but also to live our lives fully.

Red essence is experienced as strength, capacity, courage, expansion, passion, excitement, and fieriness, or the fiery power of being. Red essence is the hot blood of spirit. It is life-force. It is the energy that propels the unfolding of the cosmos. Red essence is the generative power that makes things happen. The cosmos is like a volcano, active, changing, expanding, exploding and metamorphosing. It is creating and destroying at the same time. Red essence is the generative fuel behind all of these processes.

Energy in the unified field is always in flux, always unpredictable. Outcomes are always uncertain. The cosmos is not evolving toward anything. It's just unfolding itself, exploring the infinite possibilities and potentialities of its own nature. Its unfolding takes place spontaneously. Spontaneity is one of the qualities of the cosmos and one of the qualities of red essence. Forms are always changing, appearing and disappearing. Buddha noted that the only constant is change. Accepting this reality is pre-requisite to living in the universe with reasonable comfort.

The universe is also full of wild joy and passion. Passion is a hot kind of love. The universe has this passionate kind of love. It operates with this inherent quality. It is engaged in continual metamorphosis. Everything, at every moment, is metamorphosing. The body is an ultimate example of metamorphosis, transforming from a baby to a teenager to an adult to an old person to death. We call this process aging, but it is metamorphosis. Metamorphosis is change that originates from within. We don't know where it comes from or how it works, but it changes the pupa into the butterfly and over time changes us from a toddler into an octogenarian.

The cosmos is also full of the force of expansion. It's expanding with tremendous wild joy in every direction. A nuclear explosion is a moment of pure red essence. The developments of red essence are open-ended. It is full of generative power. It is mysterious. It cannot be understood. We can get awesome glimpses of it in operation, but we cannot understand why or how it operates. We lack the mental equipment to understand it. It's like a dog trying to understand Einstein's equations with its nose. We have the wrong equipment for the job. We can only get occasional brief peeks into its operations.

Red essence is full of passion, expansion, joy, spontaneity, change, movement, transformation, and metamorphosis. All these things occur around us at every moment. This dynamic process is the way the universe unfolds itself. It is totally beyond our control. Imagine trying to control a volcano, trying to manage that hot, red lava flowing out, blowing miles high, and blowing mountains apart. It is beyond the hope of the human community to have control over that. We can only stand in awe of it.

Red essence affects human beings through a subtle organ in the chest called Rouh. This organ is the doorway to red essence. Rouh means spirit. It is considered a second heart. It is called "the Lions Heart" because its core is strength and courage. It's a heart of great capacity and capabilities, the qualities of a lion.

The Rouh is on the right side of the chest next to the physical heart. We pay little attention to heart experience in the West. We are trapped in the head. In other parts of the world, however, people focus primarily on heart experience as the path to knowledge and transformation. By learning to enter and open the heart, Being can be experienced all the way to ecstasy. Contact with the universe can be made, not by thinking or in a conceptualized way, but directly through the heart. This experience does not perceive reality and arrange it in conceptual boxes. Its nature is not describing or categorizing or noting characteristics or analyzing. In this experience, the heart contacts Being directly. It merges with the cosmos and gets a direct infusion of the qualities of Being. This infusion can produce an explosion of ecstatic experience in the heart, an ecstasy that is a primordial quality of the universe itself.

It is possible to be passionate about one's relationship with the universe, just as it is possible to be passionate about another human being. The more direct experience of essence, the more passionate one can become about it. Passion toward pure Being fuels the process of transformation.

If barriers to the flow of essence can be softened and the portal to red essence opened, consciousness will be flooded with strength. The strength will be experienced as pure capability, pure capacity, and pure confidence permeating the awareness. Questions of deficiency or limitation of capacities simply will not arise. With red essence present, capability arises innate in consciousness itself. This state is a common experience. Often, we simply know that we can do what we need to do. Difficulties may exist, but they do not generate doubts about capacities. One is rooted in capacity, and resides in strength. Essential strength supports the contemplation of projects and their execution. Life presents endless opportunities to make use of strength, no matter what our age or station, as in the case of Miriam, which follows.

Miriam was a widow in her early seventies, and she was desolate. Her only child, a daughter, was moving with her grandchild from a house down the street to New York City, where the daughter's husband had taken a new job. Miriam was unable to accept it. She was afraid of the impact that it was going to have on her life. "I never dreamed that this could happen," she said. "I don't know how I'm going to get through my old age and dying all by myself." We started to work on red essence.

In the material world, there was nothing to be done about the problem. Miriam could perhaps move herself to New York, and one day she might do so. For the moment, however, it was unthinkable to leave her life and friends of twenty-five years to go to a strange and alien city. The solution to the problem had to come from the inner realms.

Through many months, she worked on the strength of red essence. During this time, the daughter's move occurred, and Miriam was thrown into deep depression. Gradually, however, her perspective changed. Strength arose from her depths. The depression lightened. She started to go out with friends again. She resumed her life.

Finally, she was able to say: "I don't like it. I will never like it. But, I can't do anything about it. I'll do my best to accept it, and get on with my life. I may have several good years left, and I don't intend to waste them by lying in a heap and moaning. I'll cope somehow with the empty holidays and the scariness of not having a back-up in case I get sick. I have resources. I will use them." I could hear red essence in her statements.

When the Rouh opens, it opens the door to a dimension of red essence that exists throughout the universe. That dimension of Being is full of the pure qualities of strength, courage and capacity. It is the strength that gives the courage to live life fully. It gives the courage to pursue the truth. It generates the capacity to be real, without hiding for fear of the consequences of revealing oneself. It makes possible the support to try new things. This is part of the universe's quality of expansion. It is natural for humans to expand their capabilities throughout life. However, we may shut down that expansion with fear. Often, the urge toward expansion is stifled because of fear. Red essence provides the foundation, the strength, and the solidity to undertake expansion. Red essence energizes and mobilizes feelings and experiences of pure capability.

Having red essence is our birthright. Having access to the fullness and capacity of strength empowers us to cope with whatever comes up. Red essence is essential to survival and to flourish in life. If red essence is not sufficiently available, usually something has happened in the personal history to create a barrier or a veil. It is very instructive to examine the messages that were given by each parent about red essence, not only specific messages but also implied messages. Also, examine the modeling that was experienced in watching your parents interact with red essence.

The parent will almost invariably require the child to give up its strength in order to keep peace with the parent. Our structures are formed by those experiences. Bad things usually happen to us when we display strength as children. As adults, it becomes difficult to access strength. Our parents carefully trained us, and we trained ourselves, to suppress it. As adults, we keep ourselves in a condition of inadequacy by the fear that, if we exert our strength, we will be rejected. Lacking access to red essence is to be truly inadequate. It is to be deficient in the core quality that is so vital to functioning. We wind up hiding our strength and trying to manipulate our self-image, so that we do not appear to be too strong. Soon, the strength of red essence is no longer available to us.

Red essence also provides the strength to fail, and get up and try again. It's the opposite of collapse at the first sign of failure. Beneath collapse is false strength, which is not resilient. If essential strength is present, there will be no collapse. If an attempt to do something fails, the response will be to recalculate and try it another way. False strength, on the other hand, is brittle, unreliable, and crumbles easily.

Red essence gives the strength to live life fully and truly, to stand by one's being and unfold it. It makes autonomy and self-confidence possible. It provides the courage to be real instead of false, to be truly oneself. It also makes it possible to be independent, to stand on one's own feet instead of depending on others. Most important to the process of transformation, red essence makes it possible to pursue the truth no matter where the truth leads. Most of us shut down the quest for truth when it leads to a place that is unpleasant or fearful. Red essence will, over time, foster love of the truth that is willing to go toward it regardless of the consequences. The truth is worth finding, even if it is a truth that we would rather not discover.

Red essence makes separation possible. Separation is a necessity at certain moments. This could be called "healthy separation." If a person stands on your foot, it is necessary to separate from them, and say: "Get off my foot, you're hurting me." The alternative is to suffer in silence while the foot gets mangled. The metaphor can be extended. For the sake of health, strength is often required to push people away, push situations away, push life patterns away. The strength to separate arrives with red essence. It provides the strength to separate from influences that are distorting life, preventing one's unfolding, preventing one from reaching the true self, preventing one from growing and expanding to fulfill potential. This is particularly true when relationships become toxic, as was the case with Caroline.

Caroline was a young mother with two small children, two and four. Her husband was descending steadily into alcoholism. What had earlier seemed to be a minor drinking problem was quickly turning serious, and he was beginning to be abusive to Caroline and the children. She was caught in a bad situation. She came to me to deal with stress, but the magnitude of her relational problems required attention. She began work in trance on relaxation, but also red essence.

Over a year, the problem worsened. Her husband refused to enter AA, or to get help in any way. He did not think that his problem was serious, though his drinking was affecting every relationship in his life, and his performance at work. Caroline considered her options. She had worked in a mortgage company prior to marriage, and had marketable skills. She made plans to transition out of the marriage. Friends offered the use of a small guesthouse behind their residence.

With calm strength, Caroline organized herself. She interviewed for a job with a local mortgage company and got it. She arranged day-care for her two small children. Finally, she confronted her husband and told him that she was leaving. He was astounded and angry. Caroline was not triggered into anger herself. She listened to what he had to say and continued with her plans. Within a week, she was in her new place, had hired a lawyer and was filing for divorce. The separation process was not pleasant, but it was required. Caroline found the resources of red essence to carry it out in a calm and strong way.

Red essence is experienced as fullness, solidity and heat in the body. It feels as if one just got larger. It feels like courage. It feels powerful. It has generative power that is full of expansion and passion. It is also the energy that fuels self-preservation. Freud called this energy libido. Libido is red essence in the body.

The ego has its own methods of attempting to create security for itself, or assuring its survival. The ego strives for security by creating structures in the world, and attempting to fix them in place. The task of keeping forms stable in a field that is continually changing, destroying and replacing forms, is more than difficult. It is, finally, doomed to failure. We cannot keep forms in place against the processes of the universe. We must yield. We are too fragile, too small, too weak and too frail to do this job. The universe is too powerful and too massive. We can only hope to align ourselves with its processes, its ceaseless change, and live according to its reality.

Structures are not negative. The problem arises when the ego relies exclusively and blindly on structures for security—a good job, a family safety net, a paid-for house, plenty of money in the bank. If structures are assumed to be the only source of security, it must be kept in mind that part of the function of red essence is to destroy structures. In order to create new structures, old structures must go. Every structure in the world of forms is subject to destruction by red essence. So, it is risky to rely exclusively on outer structures and forms for security. The only reliable source of security is red essence. Red essence exists as the energy for self-preservation and self-renewal. If old forms are destroyed and there is access to red essence, rebuilding and renewal are possible. If there is no access to red essence and outer forms are lost, there is helplessness. Real security lies in red essence.

Red essence burns up old and decaying forms. It happens continuously all around us. Worn-out forms disappear and are replaced with new forms. The operation of red essence provides a continuing stream of fresh life and new forms.

How is access to red essence lost? We become afraid of life as it actually is. It seems too uncontrollable and fearful. We revert to the pretense that we know who we are and how the universe operates. We assume that we are in control of life. This is a delusion. We know very little. We control very little. We live in an ocean of mystery. The truth of the powerful, passionate, expansive, mysterious, and unpredictable universe is that it is dangerous. It is a hard universe to live in. It is more comfortable to create an illusory, secure universe to live in, but it is delusory. We need the illusion of safety. It assuages our anxiety and allows us to go about our business. But, the risks and uncertainty are still there, whether or not acknowledged. The big, black, mysterious and dangerous universe is still there as reality. The safe universe, which is a set of invented images and con-structs, is more comfortable, but less in contact with reality. We are afraid of life as it actually is, perhaps with good reason, so we pretend that it exists as we need it to be.

We seek solace also in rigidly structured routines. We robotize ourselves. We routinize our lives, thoughts, and attitudes. Gurdjieff called this going to sleep. He said that most of humanity is asleep. Only a few people occasionally wake up. A major way that people go to sleep is by sinking into routine. Routine seems as if it might produce a satisfactory result. The actuality, however, is that routine reduces life. It shrinks life. It can ultimately completely stifle life, because it has a numbing effect. Repetitive action is the opposite of passion, the unknown, excitement, and adventure. We seek solace in routines, not realizing that those routines dampen our experience. Rodney, in the story below, learned this lesson for himself.

Rodney was caught in a repetitious office job that he hated. He worked for an apartment database firm, and spent his days making endless telephone calls to apartment houses, asking the same five questions to ascertain current rents and occupancies. He felt numb and lifeless. He came to see me to work on depression. He had also had a series of health problems. As we talked, it seemed likely that his emotional state was slipping over into physical consequences.

Rodney was completely without red essence. He was listless, without energy or humor. His posture was slumped, and he sat sprawled. Nothing about him contained sparkle or flash. His voice was a monotone. He looked, and said that he was, continually exhausted. He was also fearful of rocking the boat by trying to change his situation at work.

We began trance-work on red essence. He was resistant. His depressed state was profound, and red essence sounded like too much work to him. We continued over a period of months. He began to change slowly. He reported one day that he had talked with his boss about moving to a better position within the firm. The boss was thinking it over. The next session, he said that the boss had decided against it.

Although that outcome was not positive, the experience seemed to light a fire in him. Within a month, he had found another position and quit his job. The new position, in sales, involved airplane travel and meeting new people. Suddenly, Rodney showed signs of red essence. His posture straightened. He seemed excited, energized and alive. He took his new-found strength into his unfolding new life.

We also stifle red essence because we are afraid of loss. We're afraid that if we allow red essence in ourselves, we will lose relationships, family, and friends. People will reject us. They won't like the real us, if we are too strong. We feel that they will only accept the familiar image that we carefully project, an image carefully calibrated to hide red essence in order to get along. We are afraid that if we allow ourselves to be real, to display red essence, we will suffer enormous losses. That probably is not true. It could work that way. If that did happen, however, it would mean that the universe was already tending toward that separation. It is unlikely that having the courage to be real will cause losses that wouldn't have occurred otherwise. Having the courage to be real opens possibilities of encountering the truth and beauty about our true self. We are all unique beings, and profoundly beautiful in our uniqueness. If we do not permit ourselves to contact the truth of who we are, then we will never be able to perceive ourselves or that beauty. It will be lost through fear of possible loss.

There's an irony here. Red essence is given up because of fear that it will lead to loss. However, loss actually occurs when red essence is given up. Surrendering red essence reduces life force, passion and excitement for living. It is the beginning of death. Red essence is shut down because we want more life, but shutting it down lessens life's possibilities. It is ironic that red essence is surrendered because it might get us into trouble, when surrendering red essence is the real thing that will lead to trouble.

It takes real courage to live life joyfully and fully, to be who we actually are, because life is uncertain and dangerous. Red essence is necessary to have courage to live fully in a dangerous universe. The alternative is to cower in place, hoping that nothing bad will happen.

Life is open-ended and has infinite possibilities. It is full of change and continual transformation. It is full of power, energy and metamorphosis. It contains freedom of movement. The future is always hidden and unpredictable, and we never know where the processes of life are leading. Death is always near, an integral part of life, part of the warp and weft of life. Life is always new, never stale, always exciting, fresh, and adventurous. When red essence is shut off, we enter into states in which the organism is not lubricated with life-energy. Loss of passion results from being severed from the hot blood of life. Without red essence coursing through the nervous system, we dry up.

The ego has little access to strength of its own. It is a carpentered-together affair. Beneath the ego is nothing but empty air. The ego knows this. It tries to mimic the strength and courage of red essence. It attempts to create strength, but can only create false strength, the pretense of being strong. False strength rests on efforting, and is mostly image. False strength does not carry the fullness and energetic power of essential strength. False strength has bluster in it. It has the feeling of a frog swelling up, trying to be ten times larger than it actually is. It remains, however, a small frog blustering. The bluster in false strength rests on feelings of deficiency and weakness. False strength is rigid. It appears the same way every time. It is mechanical. It is a process pulled together to attempt to manufacture capacity from thin air. There is no real Being in it, nothing real supporting it. There's no core of essence there. False strength involves squeezing oneself in an attempt to pull strength from somewhere inside. It is ill-constructed. It feels knee-jerk and mechanical, even to the person who's trying to muster it.

Beneath false strength is an experienced weakness, fear of weakness, and/or deficiency. It's a pretense. The statement of false strength is: "I think I can do it. I'm going to try to make myself do it." One reaches for a state in which performance can occur. However, at a deep level, capability is doubted. With true strength, the essential strength of red essence, there is no doubt about performance. The self is supported from the center of the earth. True strength is pure, living, essential, and real. It has the unlimited dynamism of Being underneath it.

False strength is one way that the ego mimics red essence. Anger is another way. Anger is blocked essential strength. It is the ego's poor and defective answer to the strength problem, the ego's substitute for strength. It does achieve some of the same goals, such as separation. Anger separates one from others, but at great cost. Anger may inflict permanent damage on relationships. If the essential strength of red essence is present, anger is not needed. Strength will do the job. It is only when strength is blocked that anger seems necessary. For many of us, resort to anger started early in life and carried over into adulthood, as the following story of Luke describes.

Luke's relationship with his parents had always been stormy. He felt that he had been over-controlled and often humiliated throughout his childhood. As a result, he was very angry with them. After he married, the parents continued to act in ways that Luke found intrusive. Blow-ups occurred, and soon Luke and the parents were not speaking, In the midst of his anger, Luke was troubled by the situation. He came to see me to work on it.

Over the course of several months, he vented his considerable anger while we worked on red essence. He came to understand that if essential strength is available, anger is not necessary. Essential strength makes it possible to speak up and tell other people what is actually occurring. Luke saw that he had hidden his feelings in the past, until anger brought about a blow-up. He saw possibilities of handling the relationship differently, more honestly, more out in the open.

Opportunity to make contact with his parents arose, and Luke took it. In his interactions with them, he expressed his feelings strongly but calmly, and told them exactly what he was willing and not willing to do. With this information, the parents were able to adjust their own behavior. While the relationship did not become perfect, it became sustainable. Luke replaced angry behavior with strong behavior. Relationships smoothed out, family holidays became possible, and life got better.

When the Rouh opens, red essence floods the consciousness and the nervous system. The sector of the personality concerned with anger, strength and confidence opens up. Information becomes available about personal issues and structures around anger, strength, self-confidence, and capacity.

Most people have constellated issues around anger, usually unconscious issues. Anger appears in the system and is vented or repressed without much awareness around the process. Anger, by its nature, always feels justified. It is difficult to step back and dis-identify with anger, so that you can see it as the aberration or bizarre behavior that it actually is.

Strength and confidence are thorny issues. The personality needs strength and confidence to live life well, but it doesn't know how to manufacture them. In fact, the personality cannot manufacture strength and confidence. The organism must have access to red essence in order to access these qualities. Women in this society have been systematically deprived of red essence by the training and archetypes that the society has imposed upon them, by the values, ideas, ideals and images that are used to socialize young girls. Many women feel that they cannot allow themselves red essence. Strength seems not to be permitted. So, many women have special problems around red essence. It's also a problem for men, but usually not as great, because the archetypes don't limit men so much in this respect.

Ego or personality is founded in deficiency. At bottom, the personality knows that it is a construction, not completely real, that is badly carpentered together. Red essence is essential to counter the feelings of deficiency. It is the healing for the feelings of inadequacy that every human being struggles with.

Ego death is a recurring phenomenon in the process of transformation. Each time a sector of the personality is exposed to understanding, the sector begins to dissolve. Dissolution of an ego structure creates inner space, and essence flows into that space. This may be a long-term process. It happens a number of times in different sectors of the personality. Ego death has its name because, from the standpoint of the ego, it feels like death is impending. This is partially true. Part of the ego is about to be dismantled. The ego's anxiety leads it to feel that the threat is to the entire organism.

There are a number of Lataif ego deaths. Each essential aspect has an ego death associated with it. Red death brings freedom from fear of people, and resolves issues around strength and confidence. The person ceases to fear disapproval from others. Red death lays the groundwork for self-trust, self-reliance and independence. The basic feeling after the red death is that, if disapproval is encountered, a task can be accomplished alone.

As adults, we misunderstand our relation to others. As a baby, our existence was dependent on our parents. We led a vulnerable, threatened existence. Our survival and continued life depended on the parents. If our caretakers had stopped approving of us and started to hate us, our survival would have been threatened. As adults, that imprinted vulnerability is transferred to society, so that we feel that it is somehow extremely dangerous to evoke disapproval. While that could possibly be true, it usually is not. As an adult, approval is pleasant but not usually crucial. If we feel that, to be ourselves, we will lose approval and be rejected and endangered, we misunderstand our relation to others. Approval is rarely necessary to survival.

The goal is to understand our true relation to society. We are each beings in our own right, with access to our own inner strength and capacity. We should not give up our connection to that inner strength in order to get the approval of a society that can withhold approval capriciously.

Finally, the red death removes the illusion of dependency. It makes us able to stand firmly in our own being. The result is inner solidity and confidence. We can be who we actually are. The red death brings a certain firm quality to consciousness. The qualities we've talked about—strength, courage, expansion, and passion—become a permanent part of consciousness. Elise, in the example below, found her strength and was able to meet her own needs.

Elise's widowed mother had recently died, leaving the family farm to Elise, her older brother, and her sister. Her siblings were attached to the farm, and didn't want to think about selling it, but Elise needed her part of the inheritance immediately. The family dynamic of long standing was that Elise's brother, as the man of the family, made all such decisions by himself. Input from the two women was not encouraged or welcomed.

So, Elise was in a bind. She needed to assert her strength and ask that her needs be met, but she felt unable to do this. She feared that her siblings' responses to such a request, particularly the brother's response, would be negative and devastating. She felt that she couldn't face such consequences.

We began work on red essence. As we worked over a period of months, Elise went through important shifts in awareness, culminating in the realization that her rights were as important as those of her siblings. Finally, she felt strong enough to write a letter and request that the farm be sold. As she had feared, her brother's response was initially negative. Her sister was ambivalent. Elise stood her ground. In time, the brother, still reluctant, agreed. The farm was put on the market and sold quickly. Elise got her inheritance, a direct result of finding the strength, the red essence, to speak up. Elise's experience is instructive. Red essence is vital to asking for what we need, setting boundaries, standing up for oneself, and functioning as an equal with others.

The Lataif is rooted in the body. It is not sufficient to grasp it conceptually with the mind. The real experience of essential aspects is located in body sensations.

This is difficult for Westerners to grasp. We are addicted to the conceptual. Body awareness has atrophied in our culture, putting body awareness outside of consciousness for most people. The unity of mind and body is a relatively new realization in Western psychological thought. The idea that the body may, in certain respects, be paramount to the mind is extremely novel, existing, perhaps, only in some schools of somatic psychology.

The mind is also useful in the task of accessing red essence, however. It can be used to examine the barriers that block red essence. It can examine what life experiences operated to shut off strength, expansion, passion, zest for life and life force. It can understand how the experiences created the barriers. Barriers to accessing red essence begin in the nuclear family. It is worthwhile to inquire into the attitudes the parents held with regard to strength, and what messages they passed along to you as part of child-rearing. These messages from your parents will have been turned into mental structures, and adult life will have been lived through the structures.

If we can see barriers, we can dissolve them. By bringing to consciousness their origin, and observing the manner in which they function, they start to dissolve, allowing essence to flow freely again. To see and understand barriers is to initiate the process of their dissolution. Awareness is the gasoline that fuels transformation.

There are few things more important to life than red essence. Without the strength to be who we truly are, to do what we need to do for the soul's development, we can neither live effectively nor transform our consciousness. The life-force needed to push through life's difficulties and create new consciousness will not be available. The more that we know about our relationship to red essence, the more red essence will be accessible to us. The more red essence that is available, the richer, more adventuresome, more powerful and more interesting our life will be.

16

Green Essence

The nature of green essence is compassion. Green essence is important because it has qualities of the heart in it. The heart is the supreme organ, the crucial core organ of the human being. It is the abode of the soul. It is very complex—multi-faceted, multi-chambered, the source of great gifts of intimacy, warmth and feeling. It is the gateway to the essential experiences of love, compassion, kindness and all the softer, open, and merging qualities. The heart enables us to contact other humans with understanding, holding, and compassion for their suffering.

Green essence flows through a subtle organ in the heart called Akhfa. The word means extremely hidden. Green essence is also active in the thymus gland. The thymus is a strange gland in the upper chest. When we are born, the thymus is large and active. It attaches and goes in among the ribs. It functions as part of growth and the immune system. It washes out disease and bacteria. This healing function is vital in surviving into adulthood. Without the thymus and its associated functioning in the immune system, children would probably not make it to adulthood.

The thymus cleanses the system. This function can be viewed as lovingkindness in bodily form, healing power in glandular form. Healing is central to green essence. Lovingkindness is having a full heart toward other human beings, toward life, toward oneself. Compassion is a deeper phenomenon and more complex.

As we mature, the thymus gland atrophies. By adulthood, it has diminished and become almost inactive. The healing and immune functions have been greatly reduced. However, the thymus can be reactivated in adulthood by re-establishing access to green essence. The organism can be washed with healing, and replenished with green essence.

When the heart is open and the heart's essential nectars are flowing freely, the Absolute's qualities of bliss, intoxication, joy, abundance, compassion, and love may be experienced. Nectars are experienced somatically as they flow throughout the body, and states are created. The cells are washed with the qualities of Being.

The heart periodically opens and closes. When the heart suddenly opens, tears usually come. Tears signal the heart's opening. It can open for any one of a dozen reasons. It can open with joy, tenderness, sorrow, grief or hurt, and tears will come. All these different stimuli open the heart, and tears can flow.

In this society, we rush to stop people from crying. It is not the correct response. Starting to cry is a moment when the heart is doing something extraordinary. Tears often lead to contact with the deeper self. Real compassion is to stand back and accept the emotion, so that the person can have their experience.

The main barrier to the openness of the heart and the flowing of its essential nectars is hurt. A specific dynamic that is part of every human being is played out with hurt and the heart. We have all been hurt many times. Hurt inflicts a little rip in the heart. A massive hurt can rip the heart so severely that death ensues. From childhood on, we experience hurt. Wounds in the heart accumulate. The varieties of hurt that can inflict wounds in the heart are practically endless. It is wounding to feel unloved, criticized, overlooked, unappreciated, or rejected. You can feel misunderstood, hated or abandoned. Each inflicts a wound that is carried forward.

The greatest wound of all is loss of essence. In losing essence, you lose access to your true being. You lose your true nature in the cosmos. Most parents don't know about essence and are not in contact with their own essence. So, they raise children who are unaware of essence. Growing children lose access to essence by observing the attitudes modeled by the parents. The result is loss of essence, generation after generation.

As a result of being wounded, we close our hearts, and construct elaborate strategies to avoid being emotionally hurt. In this culture, we consider that the worst possible thing that can happen is to be emotionally hurt. Most people will do almost anything to keep that from happening.

One of the main strategies to avoid hurt is anger. Self-righteous anger is felt instead of hurt. The strategy may work to circumvent hurt. However, the anger usually creates consequences that must be dealt with. Since hurt is a doorway to the deeper self, avoiding it at all costs may be counter-productive.

Other strategies used to avoid hurt include withdrawal, which prefers isolation to hurt, and denial, which reframes experience so that the hurt didn't happen. Hurt can also be projected onto something external to avoid experiencing it personally. It then appears to be not inside but out in the world. An example might be a fierce concern for damage to the environment, when the concern is actually being experienced personally.

The usual response to hurt is to close the heart. If the heart is closed, the battle to evade hurt may be won, but the war, having a rich, deep feeling life, is lost. Essential heart nectars cease to flow in a closed and protected heart. The heart ceases to feel much of anything. We cannot pick and choose the emotions that we are going to feel. Either we open ourselves to the feeling function and allow ourselves to feel deeply, or we close it down. If the choice is to avoid feeling, numbness takes over the heart. It feels less and less as time goes on. This is equivalent to less life, reducing life by trying to avoid hurt. Another response can be isolation from others, because they might be a source of hurt. Or, the result can be isolation from the Absolute. Closing the heart will ultimately radically reduce or eliminate full, rich and deep experiences of Being and essence. The closed heart is an enemy. To shut oneself up in a fortress to avoid hurt is to choose to live a partial life. Experiences of the joyful and the sacred will disappear, along with hurt. With an open heart, on the other hand, participation in the riches of the cosmos is available.

If hurt is permitted, it may be discovered that it is just a tiny burning in the heart. It feels like a small, red-hot coal in the heart, usually not difficult to tolerate. The strategies used to avoid hurt are themselves more devastating. Anger or rage has the potential to seriously damage relationships. The physical sensation of anger is more unpleasant than the sensation of hurt. We don't realize this. We assume that hurt is the worst thing that could possibly happen to us. We will do almost anything to avoid it.

If hurt is allowed, the burning will become cool heat, like mentholatum. The sensation will be experienced, and then compassion will come. Green essence will arrive in the heart to ease the hurt. No permanent wound will be inflicted. An open heart is a valuable thing to cultivate. It expands life's experience and depth.

Green essence is a precious nectar flowing out of the heart and through the body. The somatic experience of the nectar affirmatively answers the question: "Is life good?" The question is not conceptual. It is not answered in the mind. It is answered in the body, and the answer is yes.

When someone inflicts hurt upon us, the cause is not entirely outside of us. The pre-condition for hurt is a hole where an essential quality should be. Hurt can only manifest in the space of an essential hole. Without the pre-existing loss of an essential quality, hurt would not occur. The statement or act of the other person can only activate a wound already in the heart. For example, suppose somebody said to you: "You're worthless, good for nothing." If essential value is intact, their remark will not cause hurt. The statement will have no place to lodge. It will slide off and have no effect. The experience of hurt, therefore, points to a lost essential quality. That's important. It means that hurt can be followed like Ariadne's thread back to an essential hole in consciousness that needs to be addressed.

The major issue with green essence is the defended heart. We have been hurt many times and are afraid of being hurt again. So, we defend in a pre-emptive way. We put up walls before an attack is launched. We put ourselves on guard. We defend the heart. This makes us safe but isolated. The nectars of the heart stop flowing.

Nancy's story is an excellent example of this. An attractive woman in her mid-thirties, she wanted a relationship, but was not willing to risk it. At nineteen, she had been engaged to be married. The young man had broken off the engagement just before the wedding, and married someone else, leaving Nancy emotionally devastated and hurt. In the years since, she had kept her distance from men, although she had had offers. Now, in her mid-thirties, a man in her office had made overtures. He was lively and funny, and she was attracted to him. She was also lonely. But, she felt she might get hurt again.

We began work on hurt and compassion. Her determination to protect herself was fueling the problem. She had to be educated to a new viewpoint. We discussed at length the hard choices that face everyone, between opening up to life, risking hurt, and withdrawal from life to avoid hurt. When the choice was framed in this way, she chose, with great awareness, to live her life fully and make the foray into relationship. She was fully aware of the risks involved, and concluded that she was willing to take them. She responded to the man's overtures, and a relationship was begun. At last report, things were going well.

Vulnerability is essential to live fully. The ability to tolerate vulnerability is necessary to full, rich, deep experience. Everyone makes this choice. The heart can be defended and nectars lost, or the heart can remain open and vulnerable, the inevitable hurts can be accepted, and the riches of the heart can be experienced.

Defending can take the form of self-absorption. It is possible to become totally self-referential and self-absorbed, so that contact with others is minimal. This way of defending also stops the flow of green essence. People with heavy survival issues often choose this option. They feel constantly threatened, and that makes them self-absorbed. They cannot lift their head to get a wider perspective. Unable to truly see anyone else, they see only their own self-interest. They isolate themselves and shut the heart.

An apt metaphor for our life is a coral reef. In a coral reef, every polyp builds its own calcified cubicle. To the polyp, that calcified cubicle must be the most important thing in the world. From our perspective, however, it is the accumulation of all the cubicles that is the important thing, which makes the magnificent coral reef. Our individual lives are relatively insignificant. It's the coral reef of our combined existence that creates magnificence.

Compassion is a cluster of closely related states, all having to do with heart function. It has a number of sub-categories, such as empathy. Empathy involves merging with the other person. Their experience becomes your experience. The heart opens, and the pain that they feel becomes your pain also. Merger brings about a union of experience, a joining of field in heart experience.

A second category is sympathy. The heart is open, but less merger is present. Compassion flows, but the pain of the other does not become your pain. Green essence arrives in the system, but their plight does not become your plight. One sees the pain, and feels sorrow and the impulse to alleviate it, but does not enter it.

A third category is charity. These may sound like religious virtues. The difference is that they are not conceptual. They are attributes of the Absolute that can sweep through the body and be experienced somatically. With charity, the heart opens with a quality of good will. Blessings flow. There is no judgment, no harshness present. Positive feelings, good will, and approval flow to the other person.

A fourth category is forgiveness. The heart opens, and hurt is over-looked or relinquished. The context becomes larger than the hurt. Forgiveness, if it is real, heals wounds in the heart. Forgiveness does not take place in the head. Although the decision to forgive may be turned over and considered in the head, actual forgiveness is accomplished and fulfilled in the heart. The color of forgiveness is lime green, with a bit of the yellow of joy in it. Mixed with joy, forgiveness comes from an uplifted, open, positive place.

A fifth category is acceptance. Acceptance is similar to charity. The heart opens and the whole of the situation or the other person is embraced. Acceptance and its close cousin, surrender, are large subjects, important elements of transformation. Acceptance overcomes the ego's habitual posture of reactive defensiveness and resistance, and moves the organism closer to essence. Harsh judgment and critical appraisal are jettisoned in the process.

A sixth category is benevolence. Benevolence is a simple term for something quite profound. Benevolence appears when we understand human suffering from a vast perspective of time and space. The mind lifts above the little episodes of life, and goes to a level where the whole of human suffering is held in compassion. The Tibetans reach for a high level of benevolence when they aspire to wisdom and compassion, the two great objectives of their practices. What would the highest values of our culture be if we tried to select two? Achievement? Accumulation of wealth? Efficiency? We don't stack up very well against a Tibetan civilization that places the highest priority on compassion and wisdom.

Lovingkindness is another variant of compassion. Lovingkindness overflows the heart. It is generous. It pours warmth and connection out of a full and abundant heart. It creates a posture toward others, a particular way of viewing and relating to life and experience. It goes without saying that it has to be real. It has to arrive unwilled, as an act of grace, and course through the body. It is not conceptual. It cannot be squeezed out of the organism through an act of will. No efforting occurs with heart qualities. They arrive directly from the Absolute and flow as blessings through the body, mind and nervous system. When the green center opens and nectars flow, they bring positive feelings of kindness toward oneself and humanity in general. They bring awareness of suffering, and the truth of the harsh reality of humanity's experience.

The Tibetan Buddhists link compassion to the sacks of liquids around the brain and the heart. This sounds bizarre, but there does seem to be a liquid quality to compassion. If the sacks of liquids around the brain and heart dry up, compassion dries up. A sere quality appears when the heart is heavily defended. With an undefended heart, there is a lush, sensuous, soft, flowing quality. It is very liquid.

When compassion appears, our depth of understanding of humanity increases. We better understand, directly in the body, what humans are, what they need, and how they suffer. With that direct information, theories are unimportant. Theories of behavior and psychology are less reliable frameworks than direct experience. Green essence takes us a long way toward understanding what we need to know, without resorting to theory or conceptualization. It brings direct understanding of human experience and its pain.

Green essence is the palliative for understanding the hurts of the world and the ways humans hurt each other. This unnecessary, inflicted pain in human life causes agony for many of us. With green essence and benevolence present, we can look directly at the reality of the material world without looking away. Compassion is the way the heart renews and refreshes itself, so that it can move resolutely forward into life, in the face of omnipresent, on-going disaster. The heart expands to embrace the whole of existence.

Green essence brings freshness into life. It is a great fountain constantly flowing in the heart, delivering healing waters to parched bodies, parched souls, parched nature, and parched reality. It draws on the refreshing and renewing powers of the universe, which renew and refresh existence every instant. If we are in contact with green essence, we will not become stale or dried up. We will be washed with freshness and renewal. Human staleness, dryness, despair and desolation come not from essence but from the ego. Essential reality is never stale. In the material world, things may fade and drop away, like flowers. However, renewal comes in the cycle of new forms and new flowers. Many of us are uncomfortable with the cycles of life and death, but we might as well embrace them. The unfolding of the cosmos is structured around them. Our job is to accept reality and enjoy the ride, for as long as it may last.

Refreshment and renewal is an act of compassion by the cosmos. Freshness as an aspect of green essence is connected to the layer of greenery that covers the surface of the earth—the trees and bushes, grasses and plants. This layer of green constantly refreshes and renews the surface layers of the earth, where our life takes place and upon which our health depends.

Green essence is deeply creative and life-oriented. Qualities of the green also include delicacy and fragility. This is the delicacy of a newborn child or a budding plant. A bud that is breaking open is incredibly fresh and fragile inside. In Sanscrit, this quality is called Padma, a fresh, delicate, new quality. Padma is green essence.

Another aspect of green essence, also connected to freshness and renewal, is healing. Healing emerges from the depths of Being. Medicines and doctors may assist the process, but they don't heal. Healing itself, the renewal of form and mind, comes from deep, mysterious, essential levels. We should stand in awe that the body, emotions and mind can renew themselves through healing. Healing is a direct expression of green essence. If a damaged organ heals, it is because it has been washed with green essence. Renewal and refreshment flow from the Absolute, and the organ is made new. We don't know how this occurs, but we can observe it happening.

Essential compassion is involved with healing ourselves at the soul level. We need to come to full life again. We need to regain the splendors of Being that we have lost. By finding our true nature, we can begin to finally fulfill our vast potential. Much of the sadness that we feel as life continues is due to loss of our potential, including our potential for heart experience.

Hurt offers an opportunity. In the presence of compassion, hurt is a doorway beckoning to the truth of who you are and how you got this way. Compassion in interaction with hurt can lead to truth and understanding.

In the presence of compassion and lovingkindness, the universe seems to possess warmth. The molecules of the air seem to have warmth and intimacy. We are allowed to bathe in this wonderful sea of warmth and life. Paradoxically, green essence can also be cool. Cool green essence appears when compassion reaches great depth and becomes objective. At this level, the color of compassion becomes a deep, emerald green mixed with the black of eternity. Compassion ceases to be a human quality at this depth. It becomes objective compassion, an absolute quality. It ceases to be experienced as personal. It is from this place that one can view atrocities and say: "The Buddha smiled." This place of deepest compassion sees eternity. It sees episodes of pain and suffering on the earth's surface, but sees them from vast perspectives of boundlessness and eternity.

The ego's false substitute for green essence is sentimentality. Sentimentality is somehow too sweet, syrupy, saccharine, and overdone. We sense something false. The heart seems to be trying to be in the right place, but the emotion produced is somehow off-base, not quite real.

The ego tries continually to squeeze itself to feel acceptable emotions. We squeeze ourselves, particularly in the stomach, to try to produce out of ourselves the right emotion. We agree on which emotions are considered appropriate in certain situations, and we try to match them. When essence is operating, emotions and feelings arise spontaneously. They may sometimes arise at times that are inappropriate. Getting the giggles in church is an example. It is assumed that it is forbidden to feel what is actually being felt. Struggling to correctly match the social rules regarding emotion produces robotic behavior. Down this path, emotion becomes mechanical. The alternative is to allow emotions to flow through, without acting inappropriately. This is part of learning to be real. Even negative emotions are permitted. We are leery of negative emotions, but, like other emotions, they come and go in turn, each succeeded by another.

Allowing emotions is requisite to an open heart and a full life. The contractions that we impose, to keep from being hurt, from feeling the wrong emotion, or from feeling negative emotions, shut off life. After a few years, it can shut down most of your life. Opening to more life includes allowing the full play of the range of emotions.

The ego misunderstands compassion. Its notion of compassion is laced with sentimentality, with idealized images of saints and saviors in religion. Real compassion is very different. It is a somatic experience. It is not generated in the head, or mixed with ideas of duty or appropriate behavior. The ego's version of compassion is artificial, cold, conceptual, and forced. Essential compassion is deep, warm, and natural.

A compassionate act may not appear compassionate. This story of Khidhr, the embodiment of compassion, makes the point: One day, Khidhr was riding his horse down a lane and saw a man sleeping by the side of the road. As he watched, the snoring man opened his mouth, and a snake slithered in. Khidr jumped off his horse and began to whip the man with his whip. A crowd gathered. Then Khidhr seized rotten fruit and stuffed it down the man's mouth. The crowd objected angrily. Then Khidhr poured gallons of water down the man's throat. The crowd got exceedingly angry. Finally, the man threw up the snake, and the crowd finally understood what was happening. They saw what Khidhr had known all along, that his actions were compassionate, for the man's benefit.

Sometimes it may be a compassionate act to tell someone an unpleasant truth about themselves. Possessing the information, they may be able to adjust their behavior and avoid pain. Inflicting a small amount of pain in the present may prevent greater pain in the long term. It requires a great deal of clarity to know whether it is best to lance a wound and allow the toxicity to escape. It must be carefully mulled in the heart. The head is of no use here. The correct answer will come from the heart.

When compassion arrives, thinking stops. Compassion is not a thought or a concept, but a somatic experience. Conceptualizing pulls us away from Being, because it formulates Being into derivative thought-forms, stand-ins. We then address the derivative forms rather than Being itself. Essential experience touches Being directly. Concepts do not.

With essential compassion, fear and sadness are comforted, gathered and held by Being. Pain is seen and held. There is sadness in compassion because of the pain, but there is also a flow of healing. We are not abandoned to our pain, but held. It makes all the difference to be held and consoled in pain, and healed by Being.

Compassion is not a form of weakness. Strength and compassion can co-exist in the same person at the same moment. Think of Mother Teresa, frail and old, taking on the lifetime job of removing the dying from the streets of Calcutta. Can we imagine anything that would require more strength along with compassion?

Compassion relates to oneself as well as to others. Our culture confuses self-compassion with self-pity. Learning to hold ourselves with compassion and kindness is essential to growth and transformational work. In this culture, self-compassion is held in suspicion, as indulgent. Older, wiser cultures put it at the top of their list of virtues. Tibetan lamas who travel here are appalled at the way Westerners attack themselves. Self-compassion is necessary to provide a gentle holding for ourselves, so that we can open to life. It attends to the healing of hurt. To allow self-compassion is to accept the reality that we are all wounded, afraid, and in pain. Self-compassion provides the self with the tenderness necessary to allow wounds and fears to heal, as we see in Charles's case, in the story that follows.

As a child, Charles was sexually abused by a boy-scout leader. He felt immense shame around the memory, and felt that it was, in fact, his fault. He had never told anyone about the experience, and was unable to work with the issue effectively because it felt too shameful. It sat in his consciousness as pure pain. In hypnosis, he worked on activating green essence and applying compassion to himself. In due time, he was able to achieve a holding around the abuse experience and examine it objectively. He realized that he was not responsible. He had been a child. The man was an adult. Charles had neither initiated the experience nor desired it. He had been a victim, not a perpetrator. As a child, he had been plunged into confusion by the experience, and his misplaced feelings of responsibility had turned into shame. Seeing this, Charles was able to move past the shame and past the painful residue of the experience.

Our heritage from our Puritan history is shame. The U.S. is a shame-based culture. Shame is painful, and usually acts to obstruct inquiry and self-examination. Most people have to enter therapy to find a holding that will allow them to explore shame in their life experiences. Understanding and embracing self-compassion can go a long way toward supporting the processes that heal shame.

17

White Essence

When I entered the work, my will was in shambles. Earlier in life, I had thought that my will was healthy and reliable. I had, after all, made myself sit still in libraries long enough to get a law degree and a Ph.D. I found, however, that what I was using to get myself through life was false will, the ego's version of will, characterized by enormous efforting, super-ego override, and tyrannical self-control. False will may work to accomplish something in the short run, but in the long run it will damage your organism. Too often, it eventually crashes in burnout. That was my case. I squeezed myself unmercifully over decades to produce performance. Suddenly, one day, I could not do it any longer. My will collapsed. It simply would not respond to my instructions. I was unable to pull myself together to achieve any goal. When I reached for the resources of will, there was nothing there. It was a novel experience, and frightening, to be without an effective, functioning will. It left me feeling weak, vulnerable, helpless, and threatened.

When the teaching reached the subject of will, I saw myself in every example of false will. With real hunger, I soaked up the information on true will, the will of essence. Nothing in the work has been of more lasting importance. It was the key to surviving and getting past burnout, and it enabled me to go forward with my life.

White essence is will. The subtle organ for white essence is called Sirr. It means secret. The Sirr is found in the kath, located below the belly button. It is a center of power and dynamism. Will is generated by Being, floods through the Sirr into the organism, and prepares it for performance.

True will supports essence and the life of essence. It is important to understand the difference between true will and false will, which is the ego's substitute. The ego's version of will involves intense efforting. It is labored. The ego's answer to achievement is to apply greater and greater pressure. The ego believes in achieving by over-whelming. It seeks to end its sense of deficiency. Unlimited expenditure of effort in pursuit of achievement can destroy health, relationships, and even one's life, if unchecked by wisdom. Workaholics know all about false will. They lose themselves in work. They try not only to accomplish the job at hand, but also to end the deficiency experienced in an on-going way by the ego. This is not possible, because the source of the ego's deficiency is not lack of achievement, but the fact that it knows it is false. It realizes that it is an unreal construct, and feels ineradicable deficiency arising from its falsity. The first step toward essential will is to learn to recognize false will, along with its costs and destructiveness.

False will regards the individual as the doer. It believes unquestioningly that if anything is going to be accomplished, the individual has to do it all. The cooperative dynamism of Being is missing from the screen. False will is one of the major constructs of the consensus mind. The culture runs on false will and considers it normal. In consensus culture, false will is considered to be ambition and achievement. It is based on a strategy of trying to overwhelm the world, trying to bulldoze things by intense effort. It sees the individual as separate and independent of the context, doing battle with it.

We teach our children to overcome problems by bringing intense effort to bear. It's a mistake. With no essential reality supporting false will, it becomes an empty fiction, a mental construction. It is a set of images that masquerades as power and affects our lives. The ego knows this, and feels uneasy about will. The possibility of failure always looms large. There is always performance anxiety, an uncomfortable uneasiness about capacity. The false will, constructed from empty air, is constantly fearful of collapse.

False will is a contraction. It's a squeezing of oneself, particularly in the belly center, to try to produce results. Over time, this contraction can produce serious physical consequences for the body. False will is also brittle. When it is punched, it cracks and disintegrates easily. When false will cracks, sometimes there is no will left at all. Complete collapse of the will is burnout. It is the direct result of disconnection to Being, loss of the energetic dynamo of essence. Running on false will, effort cannot long be sustained, because the energy pool is not re-charged by Being. Progressive exhaustion will result. False will leads directly to exhaustion and collapse because there is no source of renewal in it.

The somatic posture associated with false will is the head thrust forward and the jaw clenched. The teeth are gritted in determination. The contractions of false will eventually cause problems with the head, the neck, and the lower back. The attempt is to create support with muscular contraction, which, sooner or later, damages the body. We must have the support of Being to sustain effort.

The emotional tone of false will is bravado, overlaying anxiety and fear that everything could fall apart. The ego knows that true support resides only in Being, that false will is a contraction with no reality supporting it. It knows that false will is generated by deficiency, the same motor that runs the ego. At the same moment that the ego mobilizes itself with immense effort to try to achieve something, it feels deficient and incapable underneath. It knows that it lacks the dynamism of essence.

True will is more complicated, and more difficult to understand. Its nature is solid support. Essential will has the real support of Being in it. It feels like strong hands are under the belly, supporting it. It is characterized by innate confidence and by spontaneity. There is little sense of efforting. There is no anxiety around weakness or lack of capability. The situation is observed, goals are set, and action is undertaken. Below is an example from real life, a situation that arose for a young woman named Carol.

Carol was beginning a career in voice-overs, recording the audio portion of radio and documentary movie scripts. She had good contacts and was able to get work, but she was bothered by a problem. She had no problems during rehearsals, but in the seconds leading up to actual recording, anxiety caused her to lose her breath. The problem was severe enough that it threatened to cut short her new career.

We worked on the problem of accessing essential will. She practiced putting her awareness in the belly center, and visualizing white essence flooding her system as glowing, white waters of pure dynamism and instrumentality. After a little practice, she found that she could access a state of solidity and confidence, a peaceful and non-anxious state of capability. Taking the practice into the recording studio, it worked for her. In the seconds leading up to recording, she put her attention into the belly center and visualized a fountain of white essence flowing throughout her body and mind. Her anxiety vanished. She put herself in touch with her full capacities, and performed the voice-overs without problems. The breathlessness disappeared. Her career was able to unfold without the barrier to will that the breathlessness had signaled.

With access to true will, there can be an effortless unfolding of your life. One thing unfolds out of another. Beginnings can be small and grow larger. Unfolding can proceed incrementally, with constant application but a minimum of all-out effort. It is possible to learn to flow with the unfolding. This is the sense of true will. It involves co-operating with the manifestation that the universe has already set in motion.

Understanding true will requires that you see yourself as more than a separate human being. It is necessary to see yourself in the larger context of Being, which is continuously unfolding itself. Being is the doer. Considering yourself to be the doer leads to efforting and deficiency. It is possible to slowly release the ego's conviction that it is the causative agent, along with its sense of being a separate entity. This change is at the heart of transformation, surrendering to and merging with the intelligent, alive, dynamic and compassionate field of Being all around us.

True will is made up of two parts. The first part is universal will, the will of the cosmos. The Absolute is unfolding itself in its own miraculous way. It is conscious and intelligent. There is intelligent design, even optimal thrust, to its unfolding. Consensus reality posits chaos, with no structure operative unless we impose it. This view overlooks the innate order implicit in the unfolding. Our job is to align our self with the unfolding of Being, and unfold with it. If we set ourself against the unfolding of the universe, and try to overcome it, we will jeopardize our health and sanity. The thrust of the cosmos is too powerful. The reasonable and rational strategy is to see where it's going, and assist it to go there.

The second aspect of true will is personal will. It should be kept in mind that each individual's actions and contribution are an integral part of the unfolding of unitary Being. With that caveat, we can talk about a level of universal will as personal will. Personal will involves sinking down into and occupying the body so that full use can be made of our capacities. Fear causes us to rise partially out of our bodies. We live continually with fear of death, fear of sudden disasters, fear of super-ego attack, and fear of our own deep aggressions. If the body is not fully occupied, the experiences are deficiency, inadequacy, castration and powerlessness. How could it be otherwise if essential capacities and powers are not accessible? In fully occupying the body, there is no contraction, only empowering.

Will confers the ability to take action. It includes the self-support to fail and try again, to persevere instead of disintegrating. Essential will is developed in a series of stages. First, we begin with false will, based entirely on effort. There is no awareness that anything besides personal effort is involved. There is no awareness of true will, the power of the unfolding of Being.

Step two is to become aware of Being and relax into it. Efforting is seen and curtailed. At this point, the culture and the super-ego will object that this approach is lazy. The culture will disapprove because the culture is itself built on false will. Efforting has to be reduced in order to see the possibilities of true will. Moving beyond false will, the unfolding of the universe, which occurs without efforting, becomes observable. The unfolding is vast, magical, and entirely unstrained. It is organic, like a plant growing, and its processes are metamorphosis and synthesis.

Step three moves into true personal will, a gathering of personal capacities and unfolding of potentials that are within, waiting to be manifested. Unsuspected abilities, capacities, and possibilities may emerge. Once potential surfaces, it will generate and demand further development. At this point true will emerges into the world. Dana's story, below, helps us see how this process unfolds in real life.

Dana had a chance for a new job as a facilitator for a company that presented motivational materials to employees of large corporations. The money was good. She felt that the other people in the firm would be good to work with. The only problem was that she had a long-standing fear of speaking in front of groups. This job would require presentations with microphone, screen and slides to groups of forty to one hundred fifty persons. She took the job. Before the start date, she came to me to see if hypnosis could help her overcome her fear.

We started work on white essence. In a series of sessions, Dana visualized a fountain of pure, white will, bubbling vigorously out of her belly, and streaming into her body and mind. The essential waters of will flooded her with feelings of capacity and capability, solidity, self-confidence and dynamism. As we worked over a period of weeks, Dana reported that she was feeling less fear when she thought about making a presentation.

She began the new job and spent the first few days receiving training. Then the day came for her first group presentation. Before she began to speak, she took a moment and visualized the fountain of will filling not only her body, but the entire room and all eighty people looking expectantly at her. From that moment, she felt solid and in control of the situation. The presentation went flawlessly. Self-confidence replaced fear, and she was launched on her new career.

False will is connected to old, static images. With true will, the unfolding is not into the static images of the known but into the unknown. Moving into true will, we don't know what is going to happen. We know that we are going to be different at the end of the process, but we don't know how. We are simply unfolding. Power and potential are inherent in the process. The energy of potential demands to be unfolded and developed.

The unfolding is simply followed, though it may lead somewhere unexpected. It's an exciting process. One can only see the next step. In the process of unfolding, one's true being emerges, not in images and concepts, but grounded in the reality, freshness and new life of Being.

Step four is perception of and co-ordination with universal will, the unfolding of the Absolute. Awareness of universal will is built over time. It comes first in brief glimpses. In later stages, it may be felt often. There is more experience of merger, and less experience of separateness. Isolation and separateness disappear.

The final stage is immersion in an ocean of life and unfolding potentiality. Edges are lost. Individuality disappears for periods. Ego is less present. Surrender to Being can now occur. This is an advanced stage, and few of us will get there. Our culture emphasizes personal initiative, individuality and separateness. In the West, we have additional barriers to overcome. At this advanced stage, personal will becomes less operative. The desire is to offer one's efforts as an instrument to be used by Being, to assist Being to manifest itself.

Activation of white essence is an significant step into the realm of essence. Consciousness cannot be transformed while retaining a sharp sense of separateness, of being the doer. The definition of transformation is getting beyond ego's sense of separateness, and developing an awareness of merger with the vast, rich, multi-layered and magnificent field of Being.

In spite of the ego's empty threats that life will collapse if efforting ceases, it does not. Operating with true will, the universe progressively unfolds life. There is a way of living that is deeper and more in contact with the cosmos, that relaxes fear and implements basic trust in the universe. This does not mean that we become lazy and moribund. It means that actions are carefully orchestrated to be in concert with universal will, so that the dynamo of the universe supports the efforts. The position is one of surfing the dynamism of the wave of Being, rather than relying on individual motive power to push a wagon up an endless hill. Personal energy and dynamism are put in concert with the vast unfolding already in progress.

True will is characterized by flow. It is not fragile. There is an innate sense of confidence and spontaneity in it. There is a dynamic thrust which makes things happen. It can be observed. There is nothing labored. Progress doesn't have to be hacked out step by step. There is support at each step. The unfolding proceeds one way, and if that doesn't work out, it tries a different way. Perseverance supersedes effort. The mantra of true will is: "Fall down seven times, get up eight!" Alignment is with the eternal, flowing current of life. Forward progress is generated by the dynamism of Being.

In order to grasp true will, the context of the unified field must be held in awareness. True will is a quality of the unified field. It emerges from the unified field into the world of forms. To access it, we must build an awareness of that deep unity, relax into it, and allow merger with it.

True will has an optimal thrust. Being unfolds itself in miraculous, optimizing ways that make the absolute most of possibilities. Being is ecological. It takes into account every particle in the field, weaving them all together in maximizing harmony. Every organism is sustained and nourished by its inter-actions with other organisms. Each fits into, plays its part, and functions optimally in the system as a whole. The intelligence and coordination required are mysterious and totally beyond our comprehension.

The first step in the process of will is intention. Intention arises from a longing for wholeness, a sense that something is missing and needs to be added or completed. Intentions can be generated by ego as well as essence, and they can be conflicting.

The second step is coalescence. The three centers, head, heart and belly, coalesce behind intention. Before the three centers are lined up, efforts will be disorganized, fitful, partial, fragmented, and ineffective. After they are lined up, efforts can become organized, co-ordinated and effective.

The third step is determination. Essential will begins to flow. The environment may begin to respond. Without excess effort, movement begins inexorably in a particular direction. Over time, intention, which has now become determination, will manifest something new. Potential will unfold itself into the world.

True will is less goal-oriented than ego will. True will is primarily about unfolding Being rather than reaching goals. It has the will of the universe in it. With the Absolute, no lag time exists between a determination to do something and the doing of it. The two are simultaneous. The Absolute does not make decisions. It simply unfolds itself. At the human level, there is a lag time, as we turn over possibilities, review choices, make decisions, and take action. With the cosmos, there is only metamorphosis and the unfolding of a new reality.

When ego tries to exercise will, the experience is usually attended by frustration, lack of support, deficiency and vulnerability. The efforts of false will are usually resisted by the world. Difficulties seem to crop up everywhere. Preferences are unrealized, and have to be jettisoned. The experience is of endless struggle. Through all of this runs continuous and massive efforting, as ego's attempts to achieve its goals are frustrated by an implacable or hostile world. It's like trying to sculpt a statue out of granite that resists every blow of the chisel. Effort and struggle are soon exhausting and over-whelming.

Vulnerability, fear, and helplessness may be experienced. Inside the consensus framework, this is the usual experience of false will, an attempt to wring performance out of the inadequate, limited human body. Our resources are too limited. We are too small. We cannot do it by ourselves. We cannot even perceive all the factors involved. In consensus reality, achievement is viewed as a triumph of individual will over the world. No awareness exists that the individual self is merged in a field of Being. From its mistaken perception of separateness, the ego attempts to overpower the whole system.

Achievement in the world proves ultimately to be empty. It never reaches the primary longing, which is for Being. When the first flush of successful achievement passes, the ego looks for another goal and starts the process over again. Searching the world for fulfillment does not work in the long run. The gifts of Being cannot be extracted from the world. People who achieve success in the world are often surprised to learn that it does not long satisfy their deep hunger for value and meaning.

True will rests on awareness of being embedded in Being. From the standpoint of being embedded in Being, the world looks different. It does not appear hostile and resistant. Self and world are both seen to be unfolding into new forms, new configurations, new patterns, new experiences. The major reaction is curiosity, not fear. The unfolding is seen to have tremendous power. It is impossible to predict where the unfolding, magical and effortless, will go next.

Impulses can originate in essence, including the impulse to form relationships, to change jobs, to obtain more security, to arrange life differently. These impulses are the unfolding before it hits the outer world. They should be paid close attention. The future is in them. It is wise to try to determine whether an impulse arises from ego or essence. Arising from essence, the impulse calls to be unfolded in the world. Arising from ego, it may be an attempt to counter deficiency.

The task is not to overwhelm the world with achievement, but to perceive the unfolding and assist it, to flow with the unfolding, a weaving together of inner impulses and the direction of events in the outer world. Unfolding one step at a time, with great awareness, it is usually not possible to see two steps down the road. Only the next step can be seen. Master plans that take years to materialize are usually designed by the ego. Essence is less mental, more in the moment. Master plans wind up stressing the body and producing an exhausted, contracted state that blocks access to essence.

Will is not a set of mental concepts. It is power that emerges from the belly center. It is solidity and dynamism, a somatic experience. True will feels solid and dense in the belly. There is weightiness. The lower part of the belly feels made of steel or platinum. There is a sharp awareness of self and the world. With true will, capability is not questioned. Capability is assumed. Skepticism and deficiency do not castrate confidence. The question is only: "What needs to be done next?"

There is relaxation in the experience of true will. Without the contraction of false will, relaxation becomes possible. There may be a difference in the perineum. Fear is held in the perineum, and affects the whole lower body. Even if the rest of the body is relaxed, a contraction may still be held in the perineum, if fear is held there.

Unfolding emerges from the field of Being. Although the individual is not required to do the whole thing, it is necessary to attend to your part. It is necessary to pick up the telephone and make the call. The unfolding can't be expected to take place without your participation. If true will is reached, the world will begin to cooperate. Opportunities will arise. The world will offer assistance. These are signs that true will is functioning. It pays to watch the world's unfolding closely. Our job is to weave together the world's unfolding and our personal unfolding, to sense the vast power pushing harmoniously the same way that we are pushing.

Essential will is a presence, a thereness, a state of solidity with no gaps and holes in it. Essential states contain presence. True will is an experience of presence, combined with a sensation of feeling solid, grounded and immovable. Essential will in the body translates into pure capability.

Essential will does not necessarily culminate in action. Ego will is aimed at action and achievement. Ego tells you that you have no value unless you achieve in a remarkable or noteworthy way. Action and achievement are not primary with essential will. Rather, unfolding of Being is primary. Personal achievement becomes secondary or irrelevant. Action may or may not arise out of the operation of essential will, but capacity will always appear. Essential will is pure capacity. Capacity endures and remains accessible, regardless of whether it is mobilized into action or not.

Another definition of essential will is "an intentional movement of the soul." It is a flow of deep, focused consciousness moving and strongly directed. It is soul, flowing with strength, purpose, solidity, orientation and focus.

True will produces a sense of innate confidence. It carries the conviction of being able to perform, whatever is being confronted. The ego, on the other hand, is always a little uneasy about its capabilities, and often bickers with itself. It knows that its capacities are limited, so it may argue with itself about whether or not it can do it. Internal bickering about capacity is a sign that false will is operating. Essence doesn't carry this divided conviction. Essence carries a feeling of secure confidence in capabilities.

One effect of developing access to essential will is that fear largely disappears. The familiar anxiety of ego, that a calamity will occur that can't be handled, for the most part disappears. Essential will emerges from a larger context of pure capacity and pure capability.

Essential will sees the whole picture, including the context. Extra power is available to bring to bear. It feels strong, solid, grounded, and pure. True will unfolds with less effort, so struggle becomes unnecessary. If the context will not cooperate in any way with a project, then probably false will is involved. With essential will, the context will somehow unfold and receive what you are trying to give. Only the ego will batter itself senseless in pursuit of an impossible dream that can never happen. The process of true will would give the project a try, note the implacable resistance of the context, and find a way around the barriers. True will would try something more in harmony with the unfolding of the context.

With essential will, we must watch carefully to see what the context is doing. The project needs to be somehow supported by the context as well as yourself. The myth of the consensus culture is that if we apply ourselves in a determined way, we can make anything happen. This shibboleth of the ego is derived from the Prometheus myth, which lies at the core of our culture. Prometheus was successful in his audacious goal of stealing fire from the gods. For his trouble, however, he wound up chained to a rock, having his liver eternally eaten out by an eagle. The myth contains a caution against inflated, grandiose ego goals. These goals are not courage or ambition. They are self-destructive delusion.

Essential will is indomitable. Like a wind-up toy that keeps going and turns a different way when it hits an obstacle, true will unfolds forwards, sideways and sometimes backwards until something works. It doesn't crack or collapse, as the ego may, on encountering obstacles. The solidity and capability at the core of essential will are there for the duration. True will is not brittle, but flexible and resilient. Despair is not a part of it. True will registers what is working, and adapts if necessary. Ego will, on the other hand, can go in thirty seconds from grandiosity to collapse. True will is steady, neither grandiose nor prone to collapse.

When essential will is not present, we experience the sensation of holes in the belly and in the chest. Pieces of ourselves seem to be missing. Weakness lurks somewhere in the organism. There is a body sensation of emptiness, as opposed to the solidity, fullness and groundedness of essential will. In a more advanced state of false will, ego will becomes amorphous and structureless. Nothing is left to organize itself and try again, no resilience, no power, no strength, no structure. In extreme cases, ego will becomes non-functional and incapacitated. When the disintegration of will reaches its zenith, the ego collapses into burn-out.

There are two varieties of personal will: initiating will and sustaining will. Initiating will enables us to launch something new, to initiate a project. Sustaining will enables us to sustain a program over time, even if it gets difficult. The two types of will call on different resources. The interesting thing is that some of us have an abundance of one of these varieties, but not much of the other. Some people can start projects handily, but cannot sustain them. After the initial start-up, they will walk away from the project or let it languish, so that it never fully comes to fruition. They usually wander off to start another project. They may do this for decades, going from project to project, but bringing nothing to completion. They have bountiful initiating will, but are unable access sustaining will.

Other people are the reverse. They may have difficulty launching a project, but once it is up and going, they have the resources to sustain it. These people make great office workers. They rarely attempt to start their own business, but they can keep an existing business going.

False will is conceptual. It starts in the head, and may remain in the head and never descend into the body. In this case, the body is never mobilized. Performance is squeezed out of the body, but in a context of lack of support. Awareness is focused exclusively on the personal organism. It is taken as a given that outcomes depend entirely on the capacity of this small organism. The context is almost invisible.

Ego cuts us off from Being, and leaves us feeling small and weak. To ego, the world appears as adversary, seemingly committed to frustrating preferences and projects. Tasks appear to require massive effort. There is constant fear of failure. The ego attempts to summon will in spite of these problems and deficiencies, and to override them.

With true will, any mental map held is held lightly. Acquiescence comes quickly when the unfolding takes an unforeseen direction. Preferences are lightly held, in a spirit of: "This or something better." The context is considered more determinative than oneself.

There is an awareness of openings that offer support, and the closing down of possibilities. Intelligence in the universe is assumed. Where the consensus culture sees only randomness and chaos, pattern emerges. Preferences may be frustrated, but the unfolding process continues. Surrendering to life's larger patterns is an art-form that we don't carry out graciously or well in the West.

The art of surrender can be learned in increments. It opens awareness to great forces and currents in life. Developing true will can facilitate blooming in individuals, in ways that are surprising even to themselves. Possibilities formerly not visible may become apparent. Prior planning is at the core of false will. Prior planning may shut off awareness of possibilities and flexibility to respond to unforeseen shifts. True will involves an on-going increase of awareness, an ability to respond to opportunities presented in the moment, and a willingness to surrender preferences if they cease to work. It involves learning to trust the intelligent, optimizing unfolding of the universe, which is always searching for the maximal result.

Over time, preferences may be held less tightly. Concepts of yourself may also be held more lightly. Rigid ideas about identity and capacity may evaporate. Ego's assumptions about the self are generally faulty, either too limited or too grandiose. Opening to the larger context of essential will, anything can happen. It's an exciting place to live.

The ego's process around will is stressful and tiring, particularly as we get older. When we reach a certain age, we realize that we have exhausted the ego's program regarding will. We have been this way many times, the way of efforting and grandiosity, and the side-effects are too costly. Hope evaporates that the ego's program will work. The ego is mechanical and mindless, and repeats its program of massive effort over and over again. Eventually, we cannot sustain the efforts, and decide to get off that boat. It will not take us where we want to go, and we finally realize that.

White essence has an ego death associated with it. The White Death is called "death into God." It is the disappearance of the sector of the personality typified by false will. This sector atrophies after the shift to an essential framework. In the new framework, false will feels inappropriate and counter-productive. Intimations of the White Death may come long before the shift is actually achieved. When the White Death arrives, another framework appears that places no confidence in the ego's way of handling life. The White Death brings about the transition from ego will to essential will, from false will to true will.

The White Death is a major component of transformation of consciousness. When will is seen as an unfolding of the universe rather than the ego's accomplishment, transformation is underway. With the integration of the White Death, two major lost ideas are recaptured. One is universal will, the recognition that the universe has a will of its own, which is the unfolding, the evolution of life. The other lost idea is universal law, the idea that the universe is functioning just fine. We don't need to correct it, or control it, or direct it. Of course, we cannot actually do any of these things anyway, but we give up the grandiosity of the attempts.

We are thrown up from Being for a limited time. We may allow ourselves to be used as an expression of universal will, or we can proceed with the delusion that we are solely the product of our own efforts, self-sufficient and self-contained. We are nearer the truth when we recognize that we are interlaced with all of life, and have direct access to the dynamic will and power of the field of Being.

18

Black Essence

Black essence is power. The subtle organ associated with black essence is the Khafi, located in the pituitary gland in the center of the forehead. Khafi means hidden. The power of black essence is a different kind of power from the ego's worldly power. Power in the ego's definition has to do with having power over people, control and coercion of others. It is connected to status, to having a position at the top of the political or social hierarchy, where one can control events. The ego's version of power is the ability to have your own way. Worldly power is inevitably tangled with the greed and self-concern of ego. It carries with it aggression and destructiveness. Hitler and Stalin are recent examples of men who tangled ego power with destructive ideas and brought about cataclysm for millions of people.

True black power is inner power. It has nothing to do with power over others. It is the power of annihilation of falsehood, delusion and unreality. True black essence annihilates falsehood of all kinds and opens interior space so that truth can enter. It annihilates the unreal. It annihilates false beliefs, false structures, false images, and false concepts. It is the principal ally in the endeavor to transform consciousness. If you can understand ego's structure and processes, black essence will set about dissolving that structure, creating inner space in which new essential structures can form. The possibility is evident in the story of John, which follows.

John had an alcoholic father. His childhood had been punctuated with periodic episodes of chaos, violence and family disintegration. He emerged into adulthood with a conviction that authority could not be trusted, that he had to be totally self-reliant and self-sufficient. He had had a series of jobs in corporate settings, but they ended badly. His convictions about authority made it almost impossible for him to hold a job. He was currently out of work, and came to me to see if he could change his patterns.

We began to work in trance on accessing black essence. We also worked to clearly understand his life-long patterns of behavior, and excavate the beliefs which generated them. It soon became apparent that self-reliance and distrust of authority were survival strategies for him, generated in childhood to cope with an alcoholic, abusive and often out-of-control father.

Black essence began to annihilate his false beliefs. Realizations closer to truth replaced them. He came to see that, although some authority figures cannot be trusted, others are dependable. The trick is to tell the difference. He also realized that self-reliance, which he considered a virtue, became a problem when carried to extremes. His suspicion of authority figures in general softened, and he was able to contemplate working under someone. Several months later, a job opportunity appeared. John took the new job, acting with great awareness of his issues around authority figures. The job offered him an opportunity to test his new understandings. At last report, he was dealing with the job well, and having a completely different experience.

Essential power is not dangerous to others. In the exercise of its function of annihilating the false, black essence brings the second of its qualities—peace. Black essence achieves peace by annihilating disturbance. It brings silence and peace to a turbulent mind-stream. It annihilates agitated thoughts and images, and makes rest possible. Going to sleep every night is being washed over with black essence.

In perfect peace, there is equilibrium and completeness. Nothing is missing or wanted. There is no imbalance. There is no agitation. Peace is complete just the way it is. There is no movement, no longing. We float in a sea of living stillness, silence, and peace. The black essence of Being is that sea. The power of the black is profound, mysterious, and subtle. Depth, mystery, silence and stillness are its qualities.

One of the deepest longings of the human heart is for peace. We are tossed and disturbed through a lifetime by the feverish and turbulent activities of the ego. There is no place to rest. Our minds are unceasingly agitated. Unless we can find relief by accessing black essence, our lives are filled with agitation. The ego mind is obsessive and continually unsettled around the questions: "When am I going to get what I want?" "When will my dream come true?" and "How can I be safe?" Peace cannot be found in the operations of the ego mind. The ego incessantly wants, rejects, prefers, plans, hopes, and agonizes. In its grip, we are condemned to suffering.

The ego is always moving either toward pleasure, comfort, and feeling good, or it is rejecting and moving away from discomfort. It is perennially trapped in the turbulence of these two processes. Though we long for peace, it is not a priority. Almost everything comes before peace. For most people, success, achievement, and love are all more important. Peace is at the bottom of the list. Yet, it's a quality that could make our lives instantly richer, deeper and more rewarding.

We think that we can find peace by eliminating frustrations in the outer world, but the outer world contains an unlimited number of sources of frustration. As fast as one is eliminated, another arises to take its place at the head of the list.

Peace can come only by reducing the internal activities of wanting and not wanting, desiring and rejecting. The part that wants pleasure, comfort, satisfaction and rewards is never satisfied. The wanting is itself the source of agitation. Peace is a cessation of the wanting that is roiling the waters of the mind. The grasping part of the human is full of confusions, hopes, dreams, and despair. It arrives with its wanting and agitation at the very beginning of life.

False black, the ego's substitute for true essential black, is characterized not only by mistaken ideas about power, but also by misunderstandings held in the inmost layers of the ego, in the shadow parts of ourselves. These parts have enough coherence to be regarded as entities within our makeup.

One of these entities is the jackal. The jackal is a layer of irritation and minor hostility to the world. It snaps at people. It is abrasive, frustrated, and reactive. The jackal involves negative merging. If we cannot merge with others in positive ways, then merger may take place within seething and irritation. It is possible for the jackal to continue to seethe for days after conflictive encounters, long after the other person has disappeared from view. We have all had this experience.

Below the layer of the jackal is the layer of the alien. The alien is a more serious problem, and more dangerous. It is a psychic part created by having been hurt many times. As a result of wounds, which are still hurting, it is actively hostile to the world and to other people. It is extremely reactive, explosive and unpredictable. When activated, it has two strategies. One is withdrawal into sullen isolation. The other is aggressive attack, the impulse to lash out in defense and hurt.

The withdrawal strategy we call alienation. It breaks off contact with the world. The other strategy of the alien, attack, can be very serious. The alien's attacks are much more dangerous than the irritation of the jackal. They can kill. The alien is in real pain, and it can unpredictably explode outward in aggression and hatred. Once awakened, the alien is lost in its pain, and seeks to inflict pain on others. It comes forth furiously to do battle, with anger, rage and seething resentment. It has the energy of the animal soul that fuels it. It is completely full of itself. It swims in righteous indignation, and feels entirely justified in inflicting pain on others. Its attacks are unconscious and uncontrolled, and it usually succeeds in its desire to hurt others. When the alien in one person emerges, it usually triggers the alien in the other person. Once both people are in the grip of the alien, the interaction can degenerate into furious destructiveness.

The alien nurses old grievances and wounds. It has only its two primitive responses, sullen withdrawal and furious attack. It has no middle ground. With both strategies, it breaks contact. In breaking contact lies the possibility of ending its pain. The alien is very hot emotionally.

By contrast, the beast, which lies below the layer of the alien, is cold and calculating, and even more dangerous than the alien. The beast is pure hatred, hatred of other people and of life. It is pure destructiveness, pure malice. The beast is actively but quietly destructive. It seeks the destruction of every good thing. It hates goodness, the light, all the softer human qualities. It hates everything that makes life good, decent, wholesome, and enjoyable.

The beast is dedicated to destroying everything, in order to return to perfect, black, empty peace. It seeks the destruction of all life and all of its forms. Nothing is more destructive to human life. It is a part of us all.

We know at some level that the beast is inside of us, but we do not want to turn toward it. It's too scary. We would prefer that it weren't there. The beast is part of Freud's death wish. It is located in the ancient reptilian brain at the back of the head, and also lives in the intestines. It has no compassion. It can kill without emotion. If the beast emerges in one person, it may activate the beast in another, creating a very dangerous situation. There is a collective layer of hatred around the globe because of the beast. We have to live with it. The beast emerges in wars, with atrocities tapping depths of depravity that civilized man doesn't suspect exist. The beast is not goal-oriented, other than seeking simple destruction of the good. Its mode is perverse cruelty for the sake of cruelty.

At the core of the ego, beneath the beast, is the black hole of the abyss, infinite black emptiness. The abyss is terrifying to humans. We will do almost anything to avoid encountering it. We associate it with endless falling and death. Across the globe, we are afraid of the dark. We feel that there might be something malevolent in the darkness, something demonic, destructive and dangerous. This terror is often felt in childhood. It is unreasoning. It pervades our cells. It comes from our depths. The terror is correct. There is something lurking in the darkness. It's the beast, but it is in us.

It is part of us, not out in the world. Often, destructive hatred is projected outside of ourselves, perhaps onto another group. Feeling that they should be destroyed can then be justified. We may perceive them through a lens of paranoia, out to get us, or we may be afraid of the beast in them. The projection of destructive hatred outside allows the beast to go undetected within ourselves.

The baby first encounters the beast in its parents. It is imprinted for a lifetime by the experience. In time, wounding generates the beast in the child. So it is passed down generation after generation. The beast hates the light, hates love, hates the universe, hates everything good. We sense this malevolence inside of us and it frightens us.

Our hope for getting past the false black lies in the Black Death, in which a segment of the ego disappears. The Black Death arrives when true black essence is distilled from false black essence. Struggle with oneself ceases. Knowledge that the beast is inside all of us is in awareness. Knowledge of true black essence is available, with its peace, power, and annihilation of the false. Truth is contacted, the system balances itself, chaos disappears and peace manifests. True black essence is experienced in all of it power, peace, beauty, and stillness.

19

Yellow Essence

Yellow essence brings joy and lightheartedness. The subtle organ is the "Qalb." It is located in the left side of the chest, next to the heart. When the Qalb opens, pure joy and happiness flow. Joy is an exploding spontaneity and lightness. It is felt in the heart as a series of tiny explosions. It feels as if small bubbles are popping rapidly in the heart. Through yellow essence, the joy of the cosmos makes itself accessible to humans. When essence flows through us as joy, it floods the cells and nervous system and lights them up. The atoms and cells become joy, and begin to dance.

In Arabic, the word Qalb means two things. First, it means heart. This refers to the fact that joy is a heart experience. The experience of joy and the experience of love are similar in some ways. Both are light states, highly energized. Both are characterized by excitement, happiness, even giddiness. The two states often emerge together. When we are in love, we are joyful. When we're joyful, we're close to love, and it's easy to love. In both states, the heart opens and its nectars flow.

A second meaning of Qalb is "reversal of orders." The opening of the Qalb reverses our perceptions of reality. We usually look at the world from the perspective of ego. Our perceptions are survival-oriented, anxiety-filled, distorted, and characterized by mechanical responses. Ego perceptions are built around responding to the material layer of the universe. The ego is designed to function in the physical world.

Other layers of reality, dimensions of Being, are not manifest in the physical world. The ego is not equipped to deal with those. When the Qalb opens, priorities are reversed and the inner aspects of Being, the qualities of joyful, carefree celebration, are brought to the forefront.

All priorities shift. Instead of survival, self-striving, and success, the focus shifts to abundance, love, spirit, and soft, inner states. We are captured by soul. In this state of lightness and joy, we can open and perceive the wonder of our mysterious journey through time and space. We can perceive the miraculous quality of the celebration around us.

In this state, we are filled with curiosity and joy, rather than fear. We feel delight to be alive, and part of all this. Ordinary patterns of concern disappear. In their place, the ripe fullness of joy and being alive blooms.

The first stages of heart opening are associated with the fool. This is the divine fool, found in Zen Buddhism and Sufism. The fool's actions are bizarre by social standards. The fool is so lifted with spirit, joy and inner experience that he operates on a different set of givens. Filled with a physical state of boundless joy, he doesn't care about appropriateness, or how we are supposed to act. His behavior makes him appears a fool in the eyes of the community, who are still mired in the heavy, fearful, mechanical consciousness of the ego.

Joy causes the heart to fly open, instantly shifting all ideas of reality. Joy can completely capture awareness, absorbing the organism in sweetness, fullness and deliciousness. Nothing society offers can compete with this state. Though we may have experienced little of it, we long to be consumed by the intensity and abundance of this unrestrained heart experience.

A third meaning given to Qalb is mind. The heart has a certain kind of mind. When one is sensitive and thoughtful, it is a heart function. If the heart is open, its nectars can flow. Joy, love and compassion can be expressed. While it opens, abundance can flow without obstruction. Many qualities that we consider to be mental—sensitivity to others, clarity and discrimination, recognition of the truth—have a heart quality as well as a head quality.

Joy is called "the robe of glory." It covers essential presence, the manifestation of overflowing Being. The strange thing about joy or happiness is that it does not flow if we seek it directly. It's an expression, a side effect, of harmony. It cannot be produced by determined effort. Joy is a special contact with the universe, an expression of the nature of Being. We may open to its possibility by paying close attention to our contact with Being. When it comes, however, it comes as grace, Being over-flowing with itself. An experience of joy is a direct experience of the fullness and celebration of Being.

The experience of joy in the body is intense. There is a continuum from light joy to drunken, delirious ecstasy. People in this culture long for joy, but they get little of it, and in fact are afraid of it. They do not quite know what to do with it. They fear that it might get out of control. Most people have a longing to sing, dance, and let joy flow, but they have no notion of how to do this, so they do nothing. We have few outlets in the culture for joy. In the recent past, young people created discos, but they do not access the lightness of joy. They are related to the animal soul, with pounding jungle beats and sensual dancing.

The experience of joy is lightness. The more you pass into a joyful state, the lighter you become. It's a celebrating consciousness. It's a form of love, but there is no object of the love. The sweetness in the heart radiates strongly outward. It affects other people. Joy can pass right through the boundaries of another person and fill them with joy. Joy can ripple through a crowd. It glows. It is radiant. It has a happy, carefree aspect. It is not possible to be serious, deliberate, and joyful, all at the same time. The states are at opposite poles of experience.

The ego, with its falseness, has a sense of heaviness, weightiness and darkness. Joy is the opposite. It has light and lightness in it. It makes you want to laugh. The feeling is expansive, unfolding, sweet, and radiant. Joy demands that we do something with it. It demands to be expressed. It insists that we sing, dance, write poetry, talk, laugh, giggle, make love. It spawns a strong urge to celebrate life, and the celebration state overtakes us. It seeks to go into the world to express itself. When the nectars of joy are flowing, they become both the nature of the universe and the nature of the human being.

Mild shock may be associated with joy. Most of us are numb and half asleep. Joy brings us suddenly awake with a small, electric shock when we connect with it. The doors of the heart fly open, barriers dissolve and nectars flow. There's a sudden relaxation of tension, as if bursting through the top of a box that has been restraining us for a long time. There is an explosion of energy radiating outward. We become truly alive. We could have more joy in our lives if we understood how the heart functions, and what has shut our hearts down.

There's an element of the unburdened and childlike in joy. It brings an absence of care. We associate it with children because that's the time in life when we had intense experiences of joy. As we grow into adults, we experience it less. In the grip of joy, adults may revert, and act childlike. They may giggle, snicker and become a little out of control. We only have a childlike model of joy in this culture, and we return to it when joy hits our system. As joy progresses, it can deepen into a richer experience, an inner warmth that is nourishing, sweet, and pervades every atom of our being with celebration, creativity and spontaneity.

The main issue around joy is restraint of the heart. Taught as children to restrain our hearts, our hearts are closed most of the time. In the moments when restraint ceases, the heart flies open and joy may flow. This experience should be common but is not. The heart essence of joy flows only in the absence of restraint of the heart.

Joy creates spontaneity. With spontaneity, something happens without planning or forethought. It happens before the mind knows it. It is not calculated or considered. Spontaneity is unplanned by its very nature. The heart is faster than the mind. If spontaneity is present, we act before we can think of consequences.

Spontaneity has issues of its own. It may lead to inappropriate or even destructive behavior. The whole situation must be taken into account, including everyone's feelings and interests. If we are in touch with the whole situation, we can be spontaneous but not inappropriate or destructive. Spontaneity is the direct, unimpeded outflow of Being from the heart.

With our children, we create restraint of the heart as we teach them appropriate behavior. Families and cultures are idiosyncratic in this regard. Mediterranean cultures appear to have less restraint of the heart. Germanic cultures appear to have more. If family members are often lighthearted, and there is much laughter, the children in the family will grow up having a capacity for joy. Whether joy can be experienced in a full, deep, and abundant manner depends on dissolving the barriers to joy that arise out of early family experience.

The moment the heart is restrained, joy and happiness are shut off. One of the things that we love about children is that they have not yet learned to suppress the heart. They do what they do. They say what they say. It bubbles right out of them. As they become adults, they learn to suppress the heart. Behavior becomes correct. Spontaneity disappears. Joy diminishes in exact proportion.

A second barrier to joy is the negative self-image, generated by the super ego. The negative self-image is a set of images soaked in deficiency. It manifests not only in feeling deficient, but also in feeling self-consciousness, in a pre-occupation that we are not alright, approved by the group, that we're not doing well, that people are judging us negatively. Self-consciousness also destroys spontaneity. It destroys the childlike feelings of openness and expansiveness. In their place, calculation arises, and we attempt to project an orchestrated image that will appeal to others. Joy disappears into the self-conscious responses of the negative self-image.

If we accept the deficiency messages of the super-ego, we cannot have joy. They destroy joy moment to moment. The super-ego must be brought under control to have joy in our life. The super-ego does not approve of behavior that is childlike, lighthearted, uncaring and spontaneous—the very qualities of joy. If permitted to do so, the super ego will impose a heavy judgment on those experiences and destroy the possibilities of joy. It is necessary to defend against the attacks of the super-ego, by sending back toward it a defense or counter-attack with energy equal to the energy in the attack. The super-ego can be silenced. The negative self-image can be rendered inoperative. Then, and only then, the fountain that is joy can burst open in our hearts, and flood our entire being with its delights.

20

Merging Gold Essence

Merging gold essence is love. Its organ is the heart. By nature, it is sweet, warm nectars flowing out of the heart like honey, softening the entire system and producing a special state of pleasure and joy in the nervous system and throughout the body. When merging gold flows, we can merge with the pool of Being of another person. It melts defenses and makes boundaries permeable. It renders one impressionable, capable of greater merging and more contact. It softens the shell. It eliminates fear, and produces tenderness. It heightens experiences of being seen and supported. It produces well-being, the feeling that life is good, and as it should be. A warm sense of intimacy blooms in the heart. Trust in the other person becomes possible. With permeability and the increased contact brought about by merging gold, loneliness is ended by sharing fields.

Merging gold lubricates the body and the nervous system, heals the emotions, and heals hurt. We all need regular doses of merging gold in order to live fully. Having it in our lives is vital to our health, happiness and sense of well-being. We need the loving nurture of merging gold to complete the flowering of our organisms. If a child doesn't get what it needs in this respect, as an adult there will be no ease in merging, or giving and receiving love and joy. It will grow up worried about how to please others, preoccupied with filling its holes around support. It will not have access to the sweetness of merging gold that it needs to develop, to be able to live life with love and support. Without merging gold, there is a sense of emptiness in the body, a sense that something vital is missing. There is loneliness, isolation and alienation. There is an absence of loving nurture. Love and kindness are cut off.

The ego's false version of love is neediness. In the realm of ego, people are drawn to each other in an attempt to fill their mutual holes. Often, it is mutual neediness, a case of the rocks in one person's head fitting the holes in the other person's head. Relationships founded solely on need rarely work well. When it is discovered that the other person cannot fill the deepest needs, including the need for Being, there is intense disappointment. At this point, relationships often founder.

Ego assumes that the primary relationship is with another human, and that the relationship with the other itself generates love, both given and received. While companionship is important and rewarding, relationship with another person is neither primary, nor is it the source of love. Love flows from Being. Relationship to Being is paramount. At most, the other person can be held tenderly, serving to trigger the flow of merging gold from Being.

The first experience with merging gold is with the mother, just after birth. As the baby is laid on the mother's breast, their fields co-mingle, and the baby has its initial experience of merging with someone on the outside. Previously, the baby was fully merged with the mother in the womb, as an organ of her body. The first experience of merger with the mother's body from outside is catalytic and formative. It lays the foundation for the capacity to access merging gold during the lifetime. Problems with the initial experience of merger can interfere with relationship in adulthood, impeding the ability to merge, to give and receive love.

Merging gold is not necessarily present when engaged in sex. It is independent of touching. It can flood the body and the nervous system unexpectedly, and in any setting. We can work with it consciously, if we are aware. One practice is "spooning," lying side by side curled up and touching each other, paying great attention to the heart experience. It works best, at least initially, to use this practice non-verbally and non-sexually, so that the entire awareness can be focused on the somatic experience.

Merging gold is not limited to human contact. Pets and animals may trigger its flow in the heart. It may even be associated with sweet and deep affection for unmanifest, living Being. It is impossible to lose love or be without it, because we are floating in a vast field of love just as a fetus floats in amniotic fluid. Being is full of love. It *is* love, and it is us.

21

Participation Mystique

Loss of Being is the core illness of our times. It is so universal that it is invisible to us. Consensus reality in the culture omits Being entirely. It explains consciousness as a brain function, the Lataif aspects as emotions in the individual, and identifies the ego as the self. With no place in our framework for the core knowledge of Being, the entire culture is suffering from crystallized ego, identity locked in ego as a separate entity. Crystallized ego sets this experience in stone. In the East, crystallized ego is considered to be a rare, pathological condition, which requires extreme practices to break down. In our society, crystallized ego is the norm. We are cut off from our source, Being, and all of its gifts. Trapped in crystallized ego, and without the solidity and fullness of Being available, we feel hopeless, threatened, empty and superficial. We are all ill from loss of Being, and suffering from a pandemic of despair.

Perceiving Being in nature and space is *participation mystique,* a term taken from French anthropologist Levy-Bruhl. He used the term to refer to the capacity of indigenous peoples to merge with nature, so that they sensed the living quality of their environment. We once possessed this faculty in the West. Now, it is largely atrophied, and we must re-learn to perceive Being. Since the Western framework omits Being, we rarely experience it naturally and spontaneously.

In a setting of natural beauty, some people in the modern West are still able to experience a vast presence in nature. With no context or understanding of Being, they define their experience as a simple affinity for nature. In a way, this is true. The presence of Being and the presence of nature are one and the same. Being, however, is vaster, deeper, and more mysterious than the plants, rocks, rivers, forests, and mountains of the earth. The ancient sensitivity to living Presence is still there inside of us, though deadened under modern layers of rationality, analysis, and materialism.

Sensing Being in nature involves perceiving an additional layer of existence, a film of invisible Presence and livingness laid over the objects of the natural landscape. We simultaneously perceive both the invisible livingness of Being and the natural landscape. Perception moves from one layer to the other. They are separate layers of reality, yet co-emergent. The roots of this experience are in mystical vision, which may be defined as looking deeply into the heart of Truth.

Another way to perceive Being is with the cells of the body, not with the mind. The mind is there to register the experience, of course, but the sensual experience of Being is generated in the living tissues of the body. It is as though the cells turn outward and sense into the world for presence. It is subtle, and usually over-looked, but it is definitely there. We can call it the presence of Being, the presence of living consciousness, or the presence of the ocean of dynamic awareness. It is beyond our capacity to understand it fully, but we can sense its living existence.

It is now twenty years since I found myself in crisis, and encountered the knowledge outlined here. I have no doubt that it saved my life. In those twenty years, I have continued to work on expanding my relationship to Being. It has been on the front burner all that time. As a result, my life has deepened. It has become richer. It has become Technicolor.

I have become progressively convinced that most psychological problems are spiritual problems at base. Perceiving that we live in an empty, unintelligent, and uncaring universe is enough to make a strong person ill with existential despair. This perception is a major source of pain in most of the people whom I see in my private practice. Both individuals and the society at large are suffering as a result of it.

Once I integrated the Point and the essential aspects of the Lataif into my awareness, my life changed radically. I was able to feel Presence inside my body and in the world around me. That integration was my healing. Space and the cosmos became full rather than empty. They became charged with intelligent, living Being. I was able to perceive the cosmos as an ocean of livingness, unfolding itself infinitely and magnificently in its dynamism into a vast multiplicity of forms. I could see the world around me metamorphosing eternally out of the ground of its own deep nature.

The world became re-enchanted, a place of magic, mystery, profound depth and meaning. And, finally, I belonged. I belonged to the whole strange, beautiful and wondrous unfolding of the life of Being. The cosmos, in all its dynamism and mystery, finally became home.

978-0-595-38003-9
0-595-38003-4

Printed in the United States
41468LVS00007B/1-51

9 780595 380039